THE POWER OF PREEMINENCE

To my
father and mother,
Wim and Riet Rulkens,
and my sister
Anneriëtte

Paul Rulkens

THE POWER OF PREEMINENCE

High performance principles to accelerate your business and career

2nd revised edition

Management Impact

Although the author and publisher have made every effort to ensure that the information in this book was correct at press time, the author and publisher do not assume and hereby disclaim any liability to any party for any loss, damage, or disruption caused by errors or omissions, whether such errors or omissions result from negligence, accident, or any other cause.

Editing by Dorseda de Block
Book and cover design by Douwe Hoendervanger grafisch ontwerp bno
(www.douwehoendervanger.nl)
Photo author by Marc Schols, www.mcmproductions.nl

First edition: Camelopardalis Research Press, 2015
Second edition: Vakmedianet, © 2019

Management Impact is a division of Vakmedianet

ISBN 978 94 6276 185 8
ISBN e-book 978 94 6276 187 2

Copyright © by Paul W.P. Rulkens. Maastricht, www.agrippaci.com and
Management Impact, Deventer, www.managementimpact.nl

Table of contents

Table of contents

Table of contents

Introduction

When I finished my education as Chemical Engineer, I was young, ambitious and broke. So I quickly accepted a job as a plant engineer in a big chemical plant. I felt like a kid in a candy store because I could do what many engineers are trained to do: solve problems that do not talk back. I was convinced I was on the right track for corporate success.

However, after a few years it slowly dawned on me that my peers were moving through the corporate ranks much more quickly than I was. I was flabbergasted: how is this even possible? What was going on?

This was the moment I became fascinated by a single idea: what is it that the most successful people, teams and organizations do differently when they want to achieve business and personal success in the easiest, fastest and most elegant way possible? This search for answers became a magnificent obsession for me. I studied successful people and organizations, became a voracious reader of books about personal and professional development, developed the habit of audio learning while driving in my car and attended every course and seminar I could get my hands on.

As a pragmatic engineer, I immediately applied what I learned. Based on the information gathered, I adopted the best ideas and, with simple focused actions, often got results that were staggering. I also realized that the best way to internalize an idea is to teach it to other people. I reinvented myself.

Since that time, I have been speaking, training, coaching and consulting. My subject is high performance; in other words, making successful people, teams and organizations even more successful. I have worked with hundreds of professionals, executives and business owners in more than 10 countries around the world. I have helped them accelerate their careers, while coaching them to adopt a few simple changes to move their teams and organizations to high performance and dramatically grow their businesses. I call this "Preeminence in business."

Who should read this book?

My best clients have one thing in common: they know you don't have to be sick in order to get better. They are pragmatic and always willing to test new approaches. They also know that if they do what everyone else is doing, they are not distinguishing themselves and are probably stuck. When it comes to high performance, the majority is always wrong.

This book captures the best ideas I have found to help successful people, teams and organizations become even more successful. All of these ideas have been tested at the front lines of modern business and professional life. All of these ideas have proven to work.

This book is written for two groups of people who realize that doing more is no longer the answer to having too much to do:

- The successful corporate executive and business leader looking for practical ways to raise the business bar even further, while avoiding working even more hours and taking the fun out of playing the game of business. This book provides not only a wealth of practical ideas for business leaders, but can also be the perfect gift for their high-performing employees. They understand that their business life will become vastly better when their teams become better.
- Ambitious professionals who understand that the enemy of success is perfection. They realize that the best way to grow

their business career is no longer to become even more proficient at what they already do very well. Instead, learning certain new business skills will accelerate their careers and turn
them into unstoppable goal achievers.

About this book

You will find 10 ideas in this book. I call them "big ideas," because
they have changed my life and the lives of many others, and they
have the power to change yours as well.

Each big idea sometimes looks like common sense, can actually be contrary to prevailing wisdom and may simply provide a new
angle to an existing idea. Yet, each big idea is profound by itself.

Big idea 1: The razor's edge

If you want to double your results, you do not have to become
twice as good. You only need to become a bit better in a few crucial
areas that really matter. This is the strangest business secret and it
is called the "razor's edge." It is the key to dramatically accelerate
your success in business and in life.

Big idea 2: Stepping out of the hamster wheel

In order to make use of the razor's edge, you need to step out of the
hamster wheel and start working on yourself and on your business. You do so by focusing on the only three activities with unlimited leverage: strategy, marketing and innovation.

Big idea 3: Strategy: how to achieve Preeminence

Certain business and leadership concepts will move you much
more rapidly toward high performance and Preeminence than
others. These strategic concepts are universal and can be applied
by anyone, anywhere under any circumstances.

Big idea 4: Marketing made simple

Whatever your product or professional service, clarity about the value you can deliver to the marketplace is essential for your success. I call this concept Preeminent marketing, a set of simple ideas that have the power to deliver magnificent results.

Big idea 5: Innovation: the majority is always wrong

If you do what everyone else is doing, you are not distinguishing yourself and are probably stuck. There are many ways to do things differently. This is the core of innovation. What I have found is that innovation doesn't require big budgets, long lead times and uncontrolled risks. It requires a relentless focus on breaking the standards in your industry or professional field instead.

Big idea 6: The power of strategic quitting

Doing more is no longer the answer to having too much to do. You have to let go first in order to reach out for new and better things. Your ability to succeed equals your ability to quit.

Big idea 7: Focus on performance, not potential

All big accomplishments start small: Small improvements, systematically applied in specific areas, will help you to rapidly get everything you can out of everything you have.

Big idea 8: Communicate anything to anyone

Success is never achieved in isolation. The ability to rally people to your cause starts with the quality of your communication. The quality of your communication starts with some powerful ideas to communicate anything to anyone.

Big idea 9: The incredible time machine

Time is the great equalizer. Your results three months from now are determined by how well you use your time today. Therefore, we all need to become excellent in the highest and best use of our time. You can build your own time machine with a set of practical, proven and powerful ideas to get twice the results in half of the time.

Big idea 10: Why smart people still do stupid things

In spite of everything, even high-performance people, teams and organizations sometimes show low performance behaviors. These behaviors are caused by a few very distinct thinking flaws. Low-performance thinking carries certain warning signs. Once you recognize these red flags, you will avoid getting stuck in the low-performance trap.

Each big idea chapter contains a set of practical ideas. The best way to use this book is, therefore, to read it entirely first and then pick the one or two ideas that have the biggest potential to help you most. After you have applied these ideas in your own world, come back for more.

The reason people often get stuck is not that they are doing ineffective things. Their actions are ineffective because they aren't the most effective use of their time and energy. It is the difference between doing things well versus doing things in an excellent way. It is the difference between the proper use of time versus the best use of time. It is the difference between applying reasonable ideas versus implementing brilliant ideas.

Introduction

My goal is that, after applying some ideas from this book, you will be able to move to high performance, achieve Preeminence and stand apart like a tall giraffe, surrounded by tiny field mice.

Are you ready?

Paul Rulkens
Maastricht, The Netherlands

1

The razor's edge

Would anyone care if your business disappeared overnight? Would anyone care if you left your company today? Would anyone care if you said goodbye to your profession right now?

In this case, I'm not talking about the wailing and gnashing of teeth by your employees, family and close friends. I am referring to your clients (will they panic?), your competition (will they dance in the streets?) or your raving fans (will they despair?) If the answer is "no, they will probably not notice I am gone," you might not be Preeminent yet. Preeminence means that you and your business stand out like a tall giraffe surrounded by tiny field mice.

Achieving Preeminence

In order to attain the highest pinnacle of success, you must reach the status of Preeminence. Examples of companies who have achieved Preeminence are Ferrari, Apple, McKinsey, etc. Needless to say, Preeminence is a great position to be in.

You know when you have achieved Preeminence when:
- People specifically ask for you and your business: "Get me..."
- Prospects come to you with minimal marketing. For example, you won't see many Rolls Royce advertisements, because of the brand's Preeminence. It virtually sells itself.
- The conversation is about how to use you, your product or service, not whether to use you, your product or service.
- Price is never an issue. Your availability and the availability of your product or services is the only concern.
- You are seen as a benchmark by your competition.
- You command premium pricing.
- Your ideas are copied and imitated.
- You are a thought leader in your field.

For many of us, this sounds like a lot of work -- time consuming and frankly out of reach. What if there is a proven way to achieve

Preeminence fast? The key is the fascinating concept of the "razor's edge."

The secret of the razor's edge

Even in a depressed economy, the top 10 percent of businesses and professionals in virtually all industries is becoming more successful than ever. The remaining 90 percent is either floating, treading water, or even drowning. More millionaires are being made in difficult economic times than in good economic times. And many of the most successful companies were started in a bad economy.

Why are some people or businesses wildly successful?

Some decades ago, while studying race horse performance, a group of scientists stumbled upon a fascinating discovery: in the long run, the number 1 race horse earned up to ten times more in prize money than the number 2 race horse. However, the number one race horse was less than 3 percent faster than number two. They called this strange phenomenon the razor's edge, a small, yet consistent advantage, which can result in a massive, exponential positive effect on performance and success.

What we know now is that the razor's edge is not limited to horse racing, but is equally valid for modern businesses and professionals.

Here is a little truth: wildly successful people do not know much more than you do. They also do not necessarily work longer hours than you do. They only do a few things slightly different, with a few small advantages in certain key areas, which are systematically, consistently and relentlessly leveraged. They have a razor's edge that carves a significant chasm between a business that prospers beyond imagination and a business that struggles to survive.

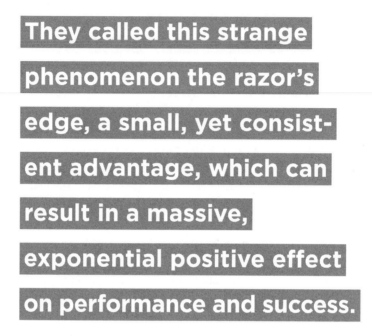

They called this strange phenomenon the razor's edge, a small, yet consistent advantage, which can result in a massive, exponential positive effect on performance and success.

Take for instance David Beckham, the soccer player. At the time of this writing, David Beckham earns an estimated 100 times more than the average professional soccer player. And yet, he does not score 100 times more goals. Come to think of it: a few years ago he retired from soccer all together and still earns 100 times more. This is an example of the razor's edge in action.

Yet, the razor's edge is not limited to the famous and well connected. It is everywhere. In my home town there is the bakery. Actually there are many bakeries, all vying for clients. Some survive, but many eventually go out of business. Bread, cakes, pastries: they are all commodities. But there is only one bakery. Tourists, as well as people from all over town patiently wait in a long line to get in this little shop, located behind a standard store front at an unremarkable corner in an anonymous part of town. The only distinction is the long line which invariably starts in the middle of the street. This bakery has the razor's edge. Its revenue is undoubtedly multiple times higher than that of its nearest competitor.

This book is all about how you can get the razor's edge in the easiest, fastest and most elegant way possible. Achieving your own razor's edge is the key to succeed beyond your wildest imagination. But first you must learn the premier secret to launch the razor's edge: future pacing.

Future pacing

A couple of years ago I saw an interesting commercial on television. This commercial was about instant soup. Frankly, there was nothing remarkable about the soup. However, in this commercial, a young manager, type A personality, had the annoying habit of loudly trying to energize and cheerlead his entire team non-stop the entire day. Exhausted after a full day of running around, he would sit down and drink his instant soup. Remarkably, after 10 minutes, his energy level was completely restored and, to the agony of his people, he'd start all over again. The interesting thing about this commercial was the young manager's catch phrase: "success is a choice."

This is a fascinating revelation. However, if success is a choice, there must be something like a master key to access it. This key can be found by taking a closer look at the human brain.

The brain is probably the most complicated thing in the universe. In the past two decades we have gained more knowledge of the workings of the brain than in the centuries before. Yet, despite this progress, we have barely scratched the surface of real brain understanding. Brain scientists have therefore developed models to describe what little we know of the brain. One model reveals that we have a conscious and a subconscious brain. And here, the quest for the razor's edge becomes interesting.

Conscious versus subconscious brain

Your conscious brain is the little voice that is constantly talking inside your head. Its main function is goal-seeking For instance, if you ask it to find the color red in a crowded room, it has no problem locating multiple sources of red. In order to do so, it will filter out everything irrelevant to achieving its goals. Thus, if you are focused on the color red, you will not see the color blue, even when looking directly at it. Likewise, we often cannot find the misplaced car keys right in front of us, because we convinced ourselves we must have placed them somewhere else. In other words: we see what we believe instead of seeing what is actually there

While your conscious brain is always at the forefront of your thoughts, your subconscious brain is a different animal, working 24 hours a day in the background. For instance, think about a time you saw a picture of a famous person in the newspaper and you could not remember her name. Then three days later, you are about to step into your car, and all of a sudden the name pops up in your conscious brain. This is your subconscious brain in action.

While your conscious brain thinks in language (the little voice inside your head), the subconscious brain thinks in pictures and feelings. A picture reveals more than a thousand words. And this is also true for the brain. The conscious brain is fast; in many ways it is still faster than a modern computer. The subconscious brain, however, is estimated to be more than 10,000 times faster.

You have a supercomputer inside your head. This is your subconscious brain. The problem, however, is that you do not always have access to this magnificent resource. Think about this: where do you usually have good ideas? Probably your answer is something like: in the shower, in bed, when I am working out, etc. If you think about it, the better question is: where do you usually not have good ideas? For many of us the answer is: "five minutes before I have a meeting with my most important client and I need to have a good idea."

If you could access and fully use the subconscious part of your brain, you would be able to dramatically accelerate your success in business and in life. How can you do that?

Accessing the subconscious brain

To answer this question, you need to travel back in time. Some 40 years ago, brain scientists asked themselves a question: how is it possible that parents of a newborn baby can sleep uninterrupted the entire night, even with the neighbors' dog barking loudly? Yet, at the moment the baby stirs and makes a soft noise, the parents wake up immediately.

The brain scientists concluded that the brain is equipped with a kind of radar, which constantly scans the world around you. The moment something important pops up on your radar, a signal goes to your conscious brain acting like a wake-up call to start to pay attention. This system works, even if you are deeply asleep.

The source of this radar is a little organ inside our brain. It is the size of an adult pinky and it is called the Reticular Activating System (RAS). The RAS acts like the gateway between the conscious and subconscious parts of the brain.

To simplify things, imagine this: the RAS is brimming with software and software code lines can be activated or de-activated. For instance, if you become a proud parent, the software line "baby cries are now important" is activated. Subsequently, you start to become aware of baby cries in your environment.

If you want to achieve success in the easiest and fastest way possible, visualize yourself already having achieved wild success.

Imagine wild success

Now consider this: if it were possible to write your own RAS software, you would suddenly gain access to the subconscious part of your brain, this magnificent supercomputer. The good news is that brain scientists have found a way to do exactly that. What they tell us is that if you want to achieve success in the easiest and fastest way possible, visualize yourself already having achieved wild success. Picture yourself already in possession of your goal and suddenly you will see yourself moving rapidly toward where you want to be. This process of imagining wild success is called "future pacing."

Why does this work? Your subconscious brain can't distinguish between a picture in your head and a picture of reality. That's why you get scared when you watch a horror movie. Since the two pictures between actual state and future wild success state do not match, it creates dissonance in your brain. Your brain starts to work to solve the dissonance between the two pictures. It starts to program the software of the RAS to become aware of people, ideas and circumstances that can help you achieve goals and alerts you to leverage these resources for your success.

Many recognize this phenomenon already. For example, at the moment you decide to purchase something you have always wanted (like a car, a handbag, a watch, etc.), you start to notice this item everywhere. Interestingly enough, the world did not change. What has changed is the way you interact with the world.

Here is the practical application to get the razor's edge and achieve Preeminence in business or your professional field: you will not know how to do it until you see yourself doing it. In other words, imagine wild success! Build a picture in your mind of you achieving your goal first. And then, by constant reinforcement, you will start to notice people, ideas and circumstances that will help you reach that goal.

The Columbus principle

Success author Brian Tracy once observed the following: when Columbus set sail to explore the New World he did not know where he was going. Once he arrived in the Americas, he did not know where he was and when he returned to Spain, he did not know where he had been.

The story of Columbus is a fitting metaphor for the way many people, teams and organizations drift through life. They have vague ideas of where they want to go. They are confused about where they are. And they are clueless about what happened to them in the past.

Thus, the essential ingredient for high performance is clarity. This is called the Columbus principle.

Clarity starts by asking: "what would I dare to do with my company, my team, or my life if I knew I could not fail?" The answer to this question is your major definite purpose: the overriding objective of all your activities. This is the place where great achievements start. For instance, if you had been working in NASA in the 60's, your major definite purpose would have been to send a man to the moon and bring him back safely. You can have only one major definite purpose. Everything else is just support.

Once you have found your major definite purpose, the next question is: "what does wild success look like?" This question will trigger you to visualize a precise picture of your major definite purpose. The more precise the picture of what success looks, feels, smells, sounds and tastes like, the easier it becomes to decide which activities to focus on to achieve it.

The future pacing technique is extremely powerful to obtain clarity and engage your subconscious mind to help you get everything you can out of everything you have.

The 10-goal exercise

Another powerful technique to avoid the Columbus dilemma, achieve clarity and become an unstoppable goal achiever is the 10-goal exercise. This exercise is an elegant way to program your brain to become aware of people, ideas and circumstances to achieve your goals in the quickest and easiest way possible.

This is how the 10-goal exercise works:
- Take a note-pad and write down your top 10 goals.
- Start with "I."
- Use the present tense, as if you have already achieved the goals.
- Use positive wording (not "I quit procrastinating," but "I am a lean action machine.")

- End with a deadline (for example "per December 2017.")
- Repeat this exercise every morning and evening, without referring to your previous goal list.

In the first few weeks your goals and wording will change every time you do this exercise. After approximately 30 days you will notice, however, that you are writing down the same goals with the same words over and over again. You now have identified the top goals that you feel most passionate about. This triggers the RAS, your pinky in the brain, to become aware of people, ideas and circumstances to help you to achieve your goals.

This powerful exercise will take less than 10 minutes per day. After about 30 days, you will notice miraculous progress on your most important goals. As a result, you will move rapidly toward becoming Preeminent in your business or professional field.

2

Stepping out of the hamster wheel

You will never get the new results you want from the things you currently like doing. If you want to achieve results you have never achieved before, you need to do things you have never done before. Becoming Preeminent, therefore, means embracing two important mindsets. First of all, you need to take full responsibility for your own actions. Secondly, you need to step out of the hamster wheel.

Me, Inc.

Let's start with a belief that's essential for your professional success, which could be success in business, your professional field or the achievement of other big goals. This belief is that you are the president of your own company. Regardless of whether you actually own your company, lead a company or are employed by a company, it is important to adopt the mindset of being self-employed. If you see yourself as the president of your own company, you suddenly have a wealth of tools to improve and grow your business, as well as the value you create for others. As president you have full control of everything that happens in your business. You decide whether you will do more, do less, start or stop activities that impact your success.

In addition to empowering you to control your destiny, envisioning yourself as president is important because your results become better only when you become better. If you are an executive or professional who wants to accelerate your career, the president mindset makes you realize the necessity of increasing value before getting a promotion.

Apart from taking control of your business and improving your own value, as president of Me, Inc. you start to associate with a different reference group. You will read different books, associate with different people and do different activities. Your reference group is a major factor for your professional success. That is why Ivy League schools are often a stepping stone for future success. While the quality of education may or may not be superior, it is without doubt the associations that catapult your career.

The person most invested in your success is you. In other words, don't expect anyone else to spontaneously take care of you, your career path and professional development. Therefore, being the president of Me, Inc. can be liberating and scary at the same time. It creates the distinction between thinking like a child and thinking like an adult. For example, you can either expect someone else to give you a raise because of seniority based on your time with the company, or you can decide to add more value first and your raise will follow suit. Only when you start thinking like an adult, will you be able to move to high performance.

Here are some immediate actions you can take to adopt the   **Act!**
mindset of being president of your own company:

- Take out your business card and strike out your current title, replacing it with "President." Carry the card in your pocket and refer to it often.
- If you are currently employed, consider your employer as your best client. Keep in mind though, your current employer hasn't always been your best client and might not stay your best client forever. Always focus on developing relationships that could lead to additional clients.
- Immerse yourself in the information used by other presidents, such as trade journals, business and professional magazines. See the appendix for a list of recommended books that could be positive resources for your professional development.

In versus *on*

What is the major secret of the high-performing 10 percent of businesses and professionals? They have developed the ability to shift time, energy and resources from working in their business, career or organization, to working on their business, career or organization. How does this work? Consider a fluffy friend: the hamster.

Imagine you are a little hamster who one day decides your goal in life is to spin your little hamster wheel as fast as possible. So you go on a diet, exercise well and practice day in and day out to reach this goal. At a certain point, you reach a level where further improvements are small and difficult to achieve. This process constitutes working in your business: becoming better and more efficient at the activities you are already doing. This is how businesses, careers and organizations get stuck.

They have developed the ability to shift time, energy and resources from working in their business, career or organization, to working on their business, career or organization.

However, the concept of working on your business is very different. Imagine you are the same hamster, with the same goal of spinning your hamster wheel as fast as possible. However, instead of jumping into the fray, you take a step back to become strategic. After some thinking, you go online and order a little electrical motor.

When the motor arrives, you connect it to your hamster wheel and it suddenly spins ten times faster than ever before. This approach translates to working on your business, and can have a profound impact on your business, career and organizational results.

The difference between working *in* versus working *on* your business separates the high-performing top 10 percent from everyone else. Once you get this, you can move to the fast lane of business success.

Let's take a look at how to apply the in versus on distinction to improve executive outcomes, accelerate your business and rapidly advance your career.

Marketing, innovation and strategy

Merely three activities define working on your business: marketing, innovation and strategy.

- **Marketing** is the process of educating the marketplace about the unique value you offer potential clients.
- **Innovation** is adding value by doing things differently than your competitors.
- **Strategy** is a systematized process for positioning your business for Preeminence and maximum success.

Marketing, innovation and strategy are obviously important business activities, but why do they make the difference between getting good results and achieving wild success? The reason lies in the potential for unlimited leverage. Marketing, innovation and strategy are the only three activities that do not have an effect ceiling. In other words, there is no limit to the impact that each of these activities can have on your business. For example, an advertisement you place in the Wall Street Journal (a marketing activity) may attract one new customer, or a million new customers.

Apart from marketing, innovation and strategy, every single business activity has a ceiling. For instance, cost cutting has a limit. Eventually, there are no costs left and additional cost cutting will have zero effect on your business. Also, keep in mind that the first 10 percent of cost reduction might be easy. After that, additional cost cutting becomes exponentially more difficult. There is simply no leverage and any effort toward further improvement is painful. This is also known as the root canal approach to business success. Cost cutting is therefore an activity that cannot be scaled up.

In versus *on*: accelerate your business

Why is making the distinction between in versus on so important? Consider this: the amount of time, energy and money spent working on your business determines the speed at which a business achieves its ambitious goals. The reason is that ambitious goals by definition require maximum leverage of everything you do. Since there is no ceiling on their effect, big business goals can best be achieved by focusing on the only three unlimited leverage activities: marketing, innovation and strategy. For example, the car maker Tesla has achieved remarkable growth by focusing on two things: an innovative concept (electric car) and successful marketing to the affluent. At the time of this writing, it is clear that further accelerated growth for Tesla can't be achieved by cost cutting, quality circles or optimizing logistics. Further growth will come from innovation (longer battery life) and marketing (attracting more and even better customers).

Since most of the time (up to 90 percent or more) in virtually any company is spent working in the business, small shifts in focus will have a major impact on the speed at which ambitious goals are achieved. For example, even in the best of companies, less than 5 percent of revenues are spent on innovation. Doubling this number to 10 percent could double (or even triple) the innovation speed.

Therefore, applying a relentless focus on marketing, innovation and strategy will help your business and yourself stand apart like a tall giraffe surrounded by tiny field mice.

In versus *on*: accelerate your career

What is true for your business is also true for your career as a professional. Thus, the fastest way to accelerate your career is to become strategic and start working on your career instead of in your career. To do so, you need to ask yourself:

- *Which professional goal would have the biggest positive effect on my business, career or organization?*
- *What is the main reason I haven't achieved this goal?*

These two questions uncover the key goal and key constraint that hinder your success. Achieving this goal and overcoming this key constraint will give you the leverage needed to accelerate your career.

Once you have answered these questions, focus on the third key question:

- *The solution to overcome this constraint is to install a system, which* ⟶ specify what exactly the system is supposed to do.

Consider for example a supply chain professional who has the ambition to advance to management. If she asks herself the first two questions, she may realize that in her case the greatest opportunity for career advancement is to forge solid relationships with senior sponsors. And the main reason that she hasn't developed these relationships is she has never taken the time to engage in relationship-building activities. Typically, her focus has always been improving skills in her profession, which is supply chain management. Realizing this deficiency, she could adopt a relationship-building system by spending 30 minutes each day on adding value to a defined group of senior executives in her company.

Systematically focusing on these three questions will help you achieve more in the next six months than you have achieved in the past six years. You're now on the road to discovering the stunning career-building power of in versus on.

In versus *on*: the final secret

So far, you have experienced the magnificent power of distinguishing between working in versus working on your business. However, real high-performance individuals know one more high-performance secret. The fast track to stunning results comes when you not only shift your focus from working in your business to working on your business, but also shift your focus further to working on yourself.

Your earning power directly correlates to the amount of value you can create for others. The value you create for others is directly linked to your skills. Any strategic upgrade of essential skills does not have a ceiling in its effect. For instance, imagine you run a successful website development company and decide to upgrade your language skills to become fluent in Japanese. Subsequently, the Japanese market opens up and you are well positioned to expand your business in this growing market.

Working on yourself starts with asking the following questions:

- *Which skill, if I would achieve it right now, would have the biggest positive effect on my business, career or organization?*
- *What is the main reason I haven't acquired this skill?*

Again, these two questions uncover the key skill and the key constraint that prevent you from making positive improvements.

Your earning power directly correlates to the amount of value you can create for others.

Once you have answered these questions, focus on completing the
third key question:

- *The solution to overcome this constraint is to install a habit,
  which* ⟶ specify what exactly the habit is supposed to do.

This statement clarifies the precise design of the solution and as
of this moment you can start building according to this design.
This habit could be to learn Japanese for 30 minutes every day.

While working with a group of scientist they expressed frustration that they had brilliant ideas to improve their business, yet
the leadership of their company did not seem overly interested. I
challenged them to ask themselves these three questions. After
extensive discussion they concluded that the missing skill was
not to get better ideas, but the ability to market ideas that were already great. After this, they committed to a systematic approach
to build, increase and use the skills to market their ideas. Shortly

thereafter, they found themselves part of board room discussions on a regular basis.

Every business skill is learnable. A simple decision to acquire the skill is all that's needed. See yourself as a work in progress and constantly build the habits to learn the critical skills for your next step to high performance.

3
Preeminent strategy principles

High-performance professionals and business leaders have very defined strategies to move rapidly toward Preeminence to realize explosive growth. These strategies are based on a fundamental understanding of business processes, human behavior and leadership mindsets.

They invariably give you the highest yield of all your efforts. Everyone can apply these strategies in the context of their business and professional fields. However, since these strategies are often counterintuitive or even misunderstood, many can almost be regarded as a secret. In other words, many competitors won't understand what you are doing. Once they have figured it out, you will be so far ahead that the only question remaining is who will become number two in your market or professional field.

Mindsets

As mentioned earlier, an effective strategy to achieve high performance requires leadership. Leadership starts with beliefs that support high performance. These are called "Preeminent leadership mindsets." To effectively work on your business and yourself, you need to understand four distinctions.

The first distinction is between everything counts versus few things matter. High-performance leaders realize that the minimum high-performance behavior they show themselves is the maximum high-performance behavior they can expect from others. They are, therefore, very clear about which leadership standards to exhibit all the time. They know that everything counts.

The second distinction is between production before perfection versus having all your ducks perfectly in a row. You need to be comfortable to launch an initiative when it's 80 percent ready. The remaining 20 percent can only be done while in motion. This is the production before perfection principle. Take for instance a cruise missile. No matter how thorough the preparation on the ground, the missile can only reach its target once it gets constant trajectory feedback after launch. Preeminent leaders understand that the enemy of accomplishment is perfection. They focus on getting their work to the world outside. In other words, to quote a renowned Apple Computing saying "real artists ship." It can be scary to bring an imperfect product or service into the world. Realize though that everything you do is a test. Every test will give a result. This result becomes input for further testing. There are no wins or failures, only results.

High-performance leaders realize that the minimum high-performance behavior they show themselves is the maximum high-performance behavior they can expect from others.

The third distinction is between the trim tab principle versus the big push. High-performance leaders see themselves as trim tabs. A trim tab is a little rudder that moves a big rudder, which, subsequently moves a massive oil tanker. It is a metaphor for the ability of leaders to change entire organizations by consistently applying desired behaviors themselves. Business success is more like a marathon than a sprint. Every overnight success is preceded by years or even decades of work. As Lord Overstone once said "no warning can save people determined to grow suddenly rich."

The fourth distinction is growth focus versus focus on everything else. Profitable growth is the essential component for any business to thrive in the long term. If an organization doesn't grow, it withers and in the end will be overrun by its competitors. If you are a business leader, growth focus should be the overriding principle of every business decision you make. If you are a professional looking for ways to accelerate your career, the best approach is to find ways to contribute as much as possible to the growth of your company. This mindset alone will set you apart from virtually all of your peers.

Needs versus wants

Imagine for a moment that you wake up with a throbbing headache and decide to go to the pharmacy for aspirin. Since all aspirin is chemically identical, you will probably consider buying the cheapest aspirin at the cheapest pharmacy that is at a reasonable distance. If you ask for aspirin, the pharmacist will give you what you want.

If, on the other hand, you go to a brain surgeon, she may conclude that an aspirin won't solve the root cause and offer a diagnosis and treatment plan instead. She is a trusted advisor and you will likely follow her lead. When she tells you what you need, considerations such as price, conditions, and timing are irrelevant, because you understand the necessity of following her advice completely if you want relief. This analogy demonstrates the difference between giving what prospects, clients and bosses want and giving them what they need.

You can make a very good living by offering what people want. I once saw a television program starring a food cop who charges $6,000 for basically coming into your house every week and throwing away all the junk food that has accumulated. Keep in mind that the food cop is an exception. Normally, if you give people what they want (such as a vacuum cleaner, car or financial services) you become a commodity and people tend to shop around for the cheapest and most convenient commodity.

Preeminence, therefore, means that you always engage in the diagnosis to find out what people need instead of what they want. McKinsey, a renowned strategy consultant, doesn't simply do what you ask (provide a sales training). Instead, the company tells you what you need in order to achieve your goals. Ironically, this advice invariably involves large investments, big commitments and the promise of dramatic results. And still clients gladly pay. No CEO has ever asked for the cheapest strategy consultant.

Strategic focus areas for Preeminence

Where should you focus your time and energy to become Preeminent in your business or professional field as fast as possible?

According to the eminent management consultant Alan Weiss, there are three areas where Preeminence is possible in relation to your clients:

- **Your product**. Preeminent products stand apart from others. They are the summit in their industries. Think of Rolls Royce in the car industry, McKinsey in the consulting industry and Stradivarius as a musical instrument.
- **Your service**. Service is the way you deliver your intangible or tangible product. For a car shop, Preeminent service can include free pick-up and return. For a consulting firm it can

be on the clock availability and for a bank it can be access to a preferred banker.

- **Your relationships**, also known as customer intimacy. How well do you know your clients and potential clients? Can you determine their exact needs? A litmus test would be whether your clients constantly surprise you, or you can reasonably predict their future needs. The latter is a sign of great relationships.

The default position for many businesses is to try to achieve Preeminence by making and delivering the best product. This position explains tools such as quality circles, focus groups and centers of excellence. However, getting the best product takes a long time, is expensive and very risky.

Fortunately, there are better ways to achieve Preeminence. Take for example Enterprise Rental Car. They have an exceptional service: they bring the car to where you are, instead of you having to go to the rental agency office.

Or take Bain Consultancy. They are good at what they do. However, their product (high end consultancy services) isn't necessarily unique. What is exceptional, however, is their relationships. The founders of Bain decided at the start to cater exclusively to CEOs. This strategy is the basis for their excellent relationships with the captains of industries in the world.

These two examples show that the biggest opportunity for any business to stand out from the crowd is to focus not so much on delivering Preeminent products, but to focus on Preeminent service and relationships.

Preeminent strategies for business growth

There are only three ways to grow a business or a professional service:

1. Get new clients.
2. Sell more value to existing clients.
3. Sell more frequently to existing clients.

Where is the biggest opportunity for your business or your career to grow? I have seen business owners, executives and professionals often focus on getting more clients as a default position to grow. This, however, is rarely the smartest approach. It often takes much more energy to get a new client than to sell more or more frequently to existing clients.

Being strategic means to focus your time and energy on activities that give you the fastest results. To grow in the easiest way possible as a business owner, professional or executive, you need to take a closer look at the following opportunities:

*   **Add new services or products** to sell more value to existing clients. For example, you can boost your product sales with a service or retainer contract.
*   **Reach out to old, dormant clients**. The reason they no longer buy from you could very well be that they have forgotten about you and your business. When approached with vigor and enthusiasm, they may gladly start doing business with you again.
*   **Start to add more value to your company**. Look for opportunities to cross functionally support your colleagues with your best techniques and ideas. Can you, for instance, let the sales department teach the purchasing department how clients buy and vice versa. Make growth the focus of everything you do.

- **Identify companies that are already catering to your ideal customers** and create alliances with these companies so you can use their customer lists to introduce your services or products. For example, very fruitful alliances are often formed between real estate professionals, movers, landscape architects and kitchen suppliers. These alliances are born from the realization of a common ideal customer: the client that buys a new house, wants a redesign of the garden, is tired of the old kitchen and needs help to move. This is a perfect opportunity to create a package deal.

Risk reversal

In any business transaction, there is always one party that carries most, if not all, risk in the end. For example, if you buy apples at the grocery store, you exchange cash for a bag of fruit. The risk in this transaction ends up entirely with you -- the apples might be rotten, acidic and full of worms -- while the grocer holds the (risk-free) cash. In this case, the risk may make you feel uneasy about the transaction or even prevent you from buying in the future.

Taking risk away from your client is one of the most powerful (and overlooked!) ways to grow any business.

Risk is, therefore, an essential part of any business transaction. Taking risk away from your client is one of the most powerful (and overlooked!) ways to grow any business. The little known secret about removing risk to grow business is called "risk reversal" and is one of the most effective strategies for Preeminence. Many preeminent organizations have made risk reversal a core priority of their businesses.

Consider Domino's Pizza: risk reversal means that the pizza is free if it isn't delivered within 30 minutes from the moment of order. The risk of this transaction has completely shifted from the pizza consumer to Domino's.

There are only three ways to take away risk from your clients or, if you are a corporate employee, from your boss:

- **Eliminate risk**: in the example of buying apples, tasting the apples before buying will eliminate the risk of discovering a faulty apple upon your return home.
- **Reduce risk**: one way to reduce risk is to let customers inspect and choose their product (such as an apple) before buying. Sampling a product is therefore a proven way to reduce risk.
- **Transfer risk**: if the grocery store could design the transaction process in such a way that it carries all the risk at the end, the client would be much more inclined to buy. For instance, the grocery store could choose to charge customers only after they have consumed all apples to their satisfaction at home.

As a professional speaker I can't guarantee the outcomes of my talks. It will depend on things like the temperature of the room, ups and downs of my clients' business and whether or not there was an open bar just before my talk. What I can control is the quality of my work. I therefore eliminate risk for my clients by guaranteeing the quality of my work. If we both agree that the quality standards haven't been met, my clients are entitled to a full refund of their investment.

What would be novel and uncommon ways to apply risk reversal in your business?

Opportunity costs

The law of excluding possibilities tells us that in order to do one thing, you can't do another thing at the same time. If you want to become strategic and use your limited resources, you need to realize you can use certain resources only once.

Our biggest overlooked resources are energy and time.

Organizational energy has a limited supply. If an organization decides to focus on cost cutting, usually an enormous amount of energy is spent to squeeze the last pennies out of suppliers and operational processes. While these efforts look successful (the savings are there), it is more important to look at this situation from an angle of missed opportunity. The cost cutting energy might have better been allocated at boosting innovation. Because innovation has unlimited leverage, if this organization had spent the same amount of energy on cost cutting, it might have realized dramatic growth instead. Few companies achieve Preeminence and market dominance by only focusing on the lowest cost.

The same is true for time.

It is therefore critical to carefully select where you would spend your precious time and energy. Since they are both in limited supply, beware that low hanging fruit might carry a hefty price tag after all.

The danger of one

The most dangerous number in business and in life is one. You are on shaky ground if you have only one supplier of goods, only one customer, only one way of making a living, and only one solution to your critical IT problem.

One generally means you are forced to play a stomach-churning balancing act, with hope as its main attraction. However, hope is not a strategy. Therefore, increasing the number one to more is a smart approach if you want to move to high performance, achieving your goals in the easiest way possible.

You can expand beyond the number one by developing options, also known as developing a Plan B. This expression isn't derived from a standard ABC list, but finds its origin in the life of Otto Von Bismarck. Von Bismarck was the nineteenth century German chancellor, famous for always having a detailed and complete back-up plan (Plan Bismarck) before starting any important negotiation.

Developing options is a numbers game. If you have no options, don't bother to waste time or energy: you are dealing with a fact. If you have one option, you have a problem. If you have two options, you have a dilemma. Only if you have three options or more do you truly have freedom of choice.

A simple way to develop options is to make a distinction between objectives (the inn at the end of the journey) and alternatives (the different paths to get to the inn). The easiest way for developing options is, once you have identified wild success, to focus on alternatives first. For example, if your objective is to meet with clients based in New York, you have multiple choices, including traveling to the meeting using public transportation, Skype, or teleconferencing.

Never be the one (there's that word again) who settles for only a single option. Leave this lazy brand of thinking to your competitors.

The positive power of negative preparation

The bigger your goals, the more resistance you will get from others. In other words, if you do not meet resistance, you are probably not thinking big enough. An essential part of strategic thinking is to prepare for and overcome resistance.

The status quo is our natural condition. We value what we already have much more than what we might gain. This condition is called the "endowment effect," which means that if we want to persuade others to take a new course of action, we will face an uphill battle. Fortunately, with a bit of effort, we can easily predict and prepare for the objections we will find on our path. This is called the "positive power of negative preparation."

The vast majority of all objections will fall in one of five categories, each requiring a different approach to overcome.
- **No trust in your character**. Trust is the conviction that the other person has your best interest in mind and is capable of helping you. If there is no trust, there is only risk. Therefore, always focus on minimizing risk. A classic example is risk reversal with a money back guarantee when purchasing an item.
- **No trust in your skills**. Others may not be convinced of your skills and experience. Also here, focus on minimizing risk. Suggest, for instance, that your clients commit to small pilot agreements and then give them the opportunity to make final decisions based on the initial successes.
- **No need for your product or service**. Other priorities take precedent. A powerful way to overcome this objection is fu-

ture pacing. As seen before, this technique is used to accomplish an inspiring future, which comes to pass only by leaving the status quo behind and executing your ideas.

- **No time**. Time is your most precious commodity. At the end of the day, you may have amassed a fortune and a legacy. The one thing that is surely finished is time. To persuade people to agree with your ideas, focus therefore on making implementation of your idea as time-saving and painless as possible.
- **No money**. There is always money. Even bankrupt companies have money. Their first impulse, however, is they do not want to spend it on your business or your idea. "No money" simply translates to "not a priority." An interesting approach is to turn this objection around and make a convincing argument such as "the fact that you have no money is precisely the reason you need to adopt my ideas, and this is why..."

Persuading others can be daunting, but the positive power of negative preparation will prove to be invaluable. However, always start with thinking about your own objections to your own ideas: the first sale is always to yourself.

Fungus, giraffe or sidekick

You are compensated according to the value you deliver to others. This is the case whether you own a business, work for an organization or operate as an independent professional. Therefore, if you want to increase your compensation, you first need to increase the value you create for others. How can you do that in the easiest, fastest and most elegant way possible?

Making yourself increasingly difficult to replace will increase your compensation.

Your compensation is based on three key elements:

- **What you do**: the nature of your work. There is a compensation ceiling in whatever you do, whether it is making hamburgers, programming computer code or being a dentist. To get paid more, you always have the option to move to a better paid job. However, doing so may require you to learn additional skills.

- **How well you do it**: the quality of your work. It is about how close you can get to the compensation ceiling in your current job. If you want to be compensated better, you have to become better. However, there is a maximum pay for people serving hamburgers (even if you are the best hamburger chef in the world!) The same applies to IT programmers or dentists.

- **How easily you can be replaced**: the importance of your work for the future of your client or your company. This is often the greatest overlooked opportunity to create value and accelerate your compensation. Making yourself increasingly difficult to replace will increase your compensation. Examples are athletes, celebrities and titans of an industry (Oprah Winfrey and Steve Jobs, to name a few).

So, what can you do to become more difficult to replace, either as a professional or as a business? Here are some suggestions:

- **The fungus principle**: build your work on a product or service that requires continuous use and replacement. A great example is SAP (an IT system for businesses). Once SAP is installed, it nearly nestles itself like a fungus inside every nook and cranny of an organization. Continuous maintenance and updates are required, and abandoning the system is costly, risky and therefore nearly impossible.

- **The giraffe principle**: become Preeminent in the eyes of your client. Once you have achieved Preeminence, the question is no longer if people will use your product or service, but how they will use it. You can become Preeminent by picking a niche and becoming the absolute thought leader in your field. For example, McKinsey has achieved Preeminence in the field of strategic consulting and Tony Robbins has done the same in personal development.

- **The sidekick principle**: step up your service level to your clients (or boss if you work in an organization) to dazzling heights. Once you decide to go out of your way to help your clients (or boss) achieve their goals and become more successful, they will become more and more dependent on you, your work and your expertise. And if they become more successful (for example, your clients grow faster than ever), you, in turn, become more successful, and you will undoubtedly be compensated accordingly. As an example, the biggest customer of Coca-Cola is McDonald's and together, these companies are mutually successful. Being a sidekick can be very lucrative and worthy. Without his sidekick Robin, even Batman would be only an average superhero.

4

Preeminent marketing principles

Marketing is the process of educating the market-place of the value you provide. If your marketing is excellent, the best customers come to you. You no longer do sales, but simply do selection, distribution and money collection. Marketing is an activity with unlimited leverage.

This chapter is about practical, proven and highly effective strategies to market your business as President of your own company: Me, Inc. These ideas can be applied in the real world, whether you are a professional, executive or business owner.

Referrals

There are several reasons why a referral from a trusted person is essential if you want to grow your service business or professional practice as quickly, dramatically and smoothly as possible.

Buying stuff is scary. We all have been burned by making a purchase that later became a major source of frustration. The overall concern is risk. As we have seen in chapter 3, in every transaction, risk is transferred from one party to the other and you do not want to be the party holding the risky bag. The risk factor makes referrals powerful. Shakespeare wrote that "the fragrance of the rose lingers on the hand which casts it." In other words, a referral from a trusted person automatically carries trust, and trust is the best antidote for risk. The bigger the buying decision, the more need for trust: no one has ever chosen a brain surgeon from the Yellow Pages.

With trust taken into account, the price of a product becomes much less important. If you know your babysitter will take good care of your children, you are much less inclined to haggle over price.

Customers who are referred to you not only buy easier, but also buy more of your product and buy it more frequently. Thus, the conversation and mindset shift from if I will use your product or service to how shall I use your product or service?

Referred customers understand the process of referrals and will therefore be more willing to refer you to others as well. The quality and process of your first sale set the expectation for the quality and process of all subsequent sales. Therefore, Preeminent professionals and businesses take good care of their referral sources and at the same time are extremely reluctant to give away products cheaply to first-time customers. They also have a systematic referrals process in place to keep the pipeline of potential clients filled.

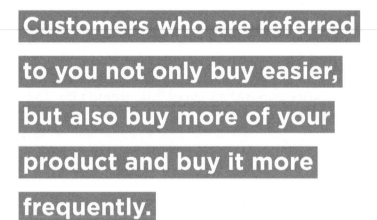

Customers who are referred to you not only buy easier, but also buy more of your product and buy it more frequently.

The velvet rope policy

Fashionable nightclubs use a velvet rope to manage entrance: only the chosen can come in. The more picky the bouncers, the longer the line of people wanting to get in. You can apply this idea to your business to become Preeminent, with several variations.

Mutual selection

Make a list of criteria that potential clients have to pass in order to do business with you. Share these criteria with new potential clients and together determine if they satisfy all criteria. Only if they do, accept them as new clients. If they don't, refer them to your competitors. In this way, you let potential clients jump through hoops to become new clients. This selectivity will make you exclusive, and exclusivity creates desire. An additional benefit is that price resistance disappears: new clients are so happy they can get in that cost is no longer an issue. This strategy to gain exclusivity is the most effective way to offer your products and services at the highest price points.

Client membership

Virtually all airlines let you earn air miles. If you have collected enough miles, there will be a reward in the form of a free ticket, free upgrade, free entrance to the airline club, etc. In order to get these rewards, you must first become a member. Airlines have found that their members are more loyal and thus buy more. Membership creates exclusivity and exclusivity creates Preeminence.

Take-away-selling

Soup Nazi was an episode of the comedy series Seinfeld that showed a long line of people anxiously awaiting their turn in a line leading to a soup restaurant. Surprisingly, the store owner was unpleasant and egregiously rude, even refusing to serve one of the Seinfeld cast. Ironically, this refusal made the soup even more attractive. In other words, human nature is somewhat perverse: we want what we cannot have.

Here is a practical application of creating Preeminence by a concept called take-away-selling: at some point, add a step to make it more difficult for prospects to become your clients. For instance, introduce an application review step to determine the final go or no go. When you do so, people will become more eager to do business with you.

Fire your customers

You will have good customers and you will have bad customers. And your worst 20 percent of customers will cause 80 percent of your headaches. Here is a simple way to make use of this fact: every year, fire your bottom 20 percent of customers. (Preferably, transfer them to your competition.) Then, use your time and energy to attract better customers. Again, you have to let go in order to reach out.

Raise your fees

The perceived value of your products or services correlates to the size of your fee. The higher the fee, the more value people think they will get. The high-end dishwasher that is twice as expensive as the cheap one is not two times better. However, it may have a razor's edge, which can be attractive to a certain group of buyers. A high price can be irresistible and comforting. No one has ever bragged about hiring the cheapest keynote speaker they could find.

The practical application of this concept is that in order to achieve Preeminence, you must raise prices and move to the highest tier possible. This action will have three major effects:

- Your margins will increase, thus giving you more opportunities for marketing and innovation.
- You will attract a certain group of buyers for which price is not an issue. And these buyers do not necessarily have to be rich. Everyone has a certain passion they spend enormous amounts of money on and are frugal with everything else. As an experiment, count the number of expensive cars in the parking lot at your nearest cheap apartment complex. There will be many.

- You will make your business resistant to major ups and downs. Both good and bad economic times will hardly impact your business. As a case in point, in the middle of the most recent global economic depression, Porsche reported its most profitable year ever.

Educate your marketplace

A recent dog food commercial depicts a veterinarian in a white coat explaining why a certain mixture of vitamins is essential to keep Bailey in top condition. This dog food, of course, is the only one which contained all these essential ingredients. This trust-building advertisement was designed to educate its customers, boosting the dog food rapidly to the top of dog food brands. Educating the market place works if you are the first one to do it and you become the benchmark in the mind of potential clients.

Act! *What can you do to educate your market place? Here are some ideas:*

- Create a special report containing information a prospect needs to know before buying your product or service.
- Give a seminar aimed at educating prospects.
- Create checklists of the most important points to consider when buying your product or services.
- Write an authoritative book about your business.

There is an even better way to become Preeminent. My daughter, who is four years old at the time of this writing, has a favorite game to play with me. She first defines the criteria of winning the game: for example, the first one who sees a person with a yellow hat, wins the game. She then fills the criteria: look, a person with a yellow hat! You understand, I cannot win this game. However, you can use this approach to become Preeminent: define the buying criteria of your business or service and then show extensively that you are the only one fitting those criteria. The first person who defines the buying criteria in your business or professional field wins!

Buy your customer

What if you could design your business so that you could spend an almost unlimited amount of money on buying customers and still be profitable. If this were the case, you could beat any competition. The good news is that buying customers is possible.

A Preeminent business is not built on many one-time sales, but on a list of loyal clients who buy repeatedly. Therefore, every client represents value over a longer period of time. This long-time worth is known as the lifetime value of a customer and it is one of the most important metrics in any business.

For instance, if you own a car dealership with a list of loyal clients, the lifetime value represents the amount of money a client on average spends over a long period of time (for instance, 10 years). If you know this amount (say $100,000) you can calculate exactly how much you can spend to get a new client to buy from you initially. This amount could be in the form of a buying incentive, a rebate or free service.

If your business is so designed to let you buy new customers, your competition will never know what happened. It goes further than this. Preeminent business owners are extremely happy if they can spend liberally on getting new customers and still be profitable. They are eager to buy new customers because the threshold for competitors to enter the market is so high that Preeminent people can easily monopolize the market.

Fall in love with your clients

One of the biggest mistakes business owners and professionals can make is to fall in love with their products or services, instead of falling in love with their clients. They become so enamored with their knowledge, technology, products and services, that they are blinded to the dynamics of the market place. This blindness is called mental myopia, which can destroy successful businesses in a heartbeat.

Preeminent businesses do things differently: they fall in love with their clients. At any given moment they have only one question in mind: how can we add more value to our clients? This question is their magnificent obsession. They know one of the biggest secrets of business: you cannot fail as long as you continue to contribute.

Move to a sweet spot

Imagine you are going to open a restaurant. And imagine that of all the advantages you can have, you are allowed to pick one. Which advantage would you choose to make your new business as successful as possible? Would it be a top chef, the best location or a famous brand?

My answer would be a hungry crowd. With a hungry crowd, you do not need any other advantage to be successful.

This distinction is important to becoming Preeminent: always gravitate toward prospects who desperately need what you have to offer. Avoid the opposite, which is trying to persuade indifferent prospects of the value of your service or your products.

Here are two practical applications of this principle for you and your business:
- Seek out and listen to your raving fans. Ignore the rest. Ask for introductions and referrals.

- Test a lot. See what sticks. Then do more of what sticks. This is a simple formula for success.

The magic of a customer list

Remember the three ways to grow any business:

- Get new customers.
- Sell more to existing customers.
- Sell more frequently to existing customers.

With this in mind, the Preeminent strategy for growth becomes simple: get more customers who will continue to buy more expensive products more frequently.

The biggest opportunity for any business is hidden in its existing customer list

Be aware that this approach does not necessarily translate to putting all your energy into getting more new customers: it is much more difficult to persuade a new prospect to buy from you than to sell more and more frequently to existing customers. This is a profound distinction with the following implications:

- The biggest opportunity for any business is hidden in its existing customer list.
- The most important asset of any business is not its products, people, equipment or intellectual property. The most important asset of any business is its customer list.
- Your first priority to become Preeminent is therefore to build, maintain and expand your customer list.

Once you have built your customer list, you can engage your customers on a regular basis for referrals, additional offers and feedback.

5

Preeminent innovation principles

Innovation is the lifeblood of any company. Without innovation, going out of business is inevitable. However, innovation can be scary, because it is often considered risky, expensive and slow to realize positive results. These perceived drawbacks of innovation are, however, a myth. To understand why, we need to make a distinction between invention and innovation.

Inventions are based on new products, like iPads, cars and washing machines. Inventing, designing and manufacturing new products are indeed risky and expensive activities that require a long horizon.

Innovation, on the other hand, involves doing things differently, which has a major positive impact on the marketplace. Innovation helps us get everything we can out of everything we have. The good news is that the vast number of business successes aren't driven by invention, but by innovation. Think of success stories such as FedEx, Amazon and Google.

This chapter is about learning how you can systematically engage in innovation to become Preeminent in your business or professional field.

Why the majority is always wrong

The great Roman Emperor Marcus Aurelius once said "the object of life isn't to be on the side of the majority, but to escape finding oneself in the ranks of the insane."

When it comes to high performance, the majority is always wrong. If the majority would be right, a celebrity like Lady Gaga, Lionel Messi or Brad Pitt (take your pick) would have been installed as world president by now. Humans have a bias for groupthink and, as a result, often readily accept any prevailing wisdom from the crowd.

You can skillfully use this knowledge to rapidly innovate in your business or professional field.

Every business or profession has industry or professional standards also known as norms. Examples of these norms are car dealers who must have a great sight location and real estate agents who use a fixed amount of the house listing price as commission.

"Norm" is an abbreviation for normal. If you do what is normal in your industry or profession, you do what everybody is doing and you will get the results everybody is getting as well. These predictable outcomes are called average results. Innovation, on the other hand, is aimed at getting exceptional results.

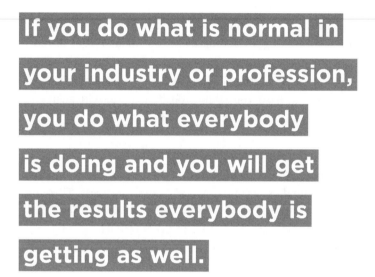

If you do what is normal in your industry or profession, you do what everybody is doing and you will get the results everybody is getting as well.

Take, for example, the curious case of London taxi drivers. If you want to become a taxi driver in London, you need to know the entire city by heart. This job requirement is known as the knowledge, which takes several years to acquire. The knowledge requirement created a problem for a taxi company some years ago that wanted to grow rapidly in the city. The company convened a think tank and asked themselves one question: "how can we grow our taxi business in London with taxi drivers who don't know the city?"

They came up with an ingenious solution. They created two different taxis: one was the standard taxi and the other had a sign that read in big, bold letters: "The driver of this vehicle does not know anything about the City of London and loves to get driving directions from you!" This brilliant move attracted people who lived in London, knew the city well and looked forward to the opportunity to play the boss in a taxi.

Rapid innovation starts with asking the right question, focused on breaking the standards in your industry. For instance, if you are in the furniture business, a question could be "what if I could no longer assemble furniture for my customers?" If you think long and hard, you would probably come up with an innovative business approach as pioneered by IKEA.

Breaking industry standards

Innovation requires focus. The default position of any organization is to mindlessly continue to work in its business. Therefore, you require an effective process to systematically look for innovation opportunities to continue to reinvent yourself.

Breaking industry standards is a technique, where you systematically use industry or professional norms to rapidly innovate and stand apart from the herd.

Follow these tips to apply the breaking industry standards technique:

- List the 10 to 20 standards in your industry or profession. For example, an industry standard for consultants is to bill by the hour.

- Imagine that, for whatever reason, it is no longer possible to adhere to one of these standards. For instance, imagine you're a consultant who can no longer bill by the hour.

- Become creative and ask yourself how you would operate under these conditions. Take a close look at how other industries or professions operate. In this consultant example, you could use the model applied in sports: a race car driver isn't paid by the hour, but paid for getting results. As a consultant you could choose to be paid by results as well.
- See how you can apply this in your world. If you're a consultant, or any other professional, start using a fixed price to get a certain result. You will notice that this innovative approach will often give you additional benefits as well. Think about it: No one has ever asked for the cheapest race car driver.

Consensus is always overrated. Next time you hear the word consensus, consider it a great opportunity to do things differently, become Preeminent and stand apart like a tall giraffe surrounded by tiny field mice.

Portable memory bank

Innovation requires getting and capturing good ideas. Getting good ideas is a numbers game. We need a thousand bad, crazy and mediocre ideas to get one really good idea. Fortunately, getting a thousand ideas isn't difficult, because the subconscious part of your mind already operates as a massive idea generator. Brain scientists estimate that you receive approximately 10,000 random thoughts from the subconscious mind every day. Unfortunately, you are consciously aware of only a fraction of these thoughts. And even if you're made aware of these thoughts, usually you have forgotten the idea 10 minutes later. Think of all the interesting ideas that have escaped your memory in this short time.

Here is a simple method called the "portable memory bank"
to help you capitalize on your good ideas:

- Carry a pen and notebook with you all the time.
- As soon as an idea pops up in your head, write it down immediately. Don't judge the idea on its merit or value. Most of these ideas will be crazy, weird or both.
- If you become proficient at this method, you can collect close to 50 ideas a day.
- After 500 ideas (in just 10 days) review all the ideas by searching for a pattern and identifying the most promising ideas.
- Take action on these good ideas immediately. Oftentimes, these are little pearls of wisdom that help you achieve your major goals faster.

Freenoting

Another way of getting new and good ideas is known as "freenoting." The vast majority of brain activity is hidden in the background of the subconscious mind. This hidden activity is responsible for emotions and feelings, and triggers dreams while you sleep. It is also responsible for creative ideas and intuitive solutions.

This ability stems from your brain's virtually unlimited storage capacity that contains your life experiences. You often have difficulty consciously accessing this memory bank. For example, how much information can you retain from history exams you took a long time ago? When a memory recall happens, it is spontaneous. (Wow, I just had an excellent idea!). Since the thoughts from the subconscious mind don't appear in logical form or order, it is up to the conscious mind to try to make sense of these thoughts. This is a difficult task, interfering with day-to-day activities. Most of the time we therefore simply ignore the thought stream coming from the subconscious mind. Is it possible to develop more control of the workings of the subconscious mind for purposes such as creative idea generation?

The answer is yes. An effective, though curious technique to make this happen is freenoting. Freenoting is a process used to put the seemingly random musings of the subconscious part of the brain in writing. After writing down the ideas, you then evaluate what you have written, picking out the gold nuggets that are the building blocks of great ideas.

Here is how freenoting works:

Act!

- Start with a question, such as "how can I increase revenue of my business?"
- Continue to immediately write down thoughts as they enter your mind. These thoughts may be strange, different and seemingly unrelated: the subconscious mind produces more than a dozen thoughts every minute. However, don't stop writing and do not interpret what you have written yet. The subconscious image stream is triggered by speed and, therefore, the speed of writing is essential.
- Continue this writing process for at least 15 minutes.
- After 15 minutes review what you have written and circle the most creative connections and promising ideas. These will be the golden nuggets that help you find interesting answers to your question.

The 20 ways thinking technique

Next to freenoting, the "20 ways thinking technique" is a practical way to continue to get new ideas. It is based on the observation that the act of thinking requires a lot of energy. Therefore, your brain develops automatic thinking patterns when faced with a problem. Getting new and original solutions for problems is therefore difficult.

The 20 ways thinking technique is a quick way to bypass these mental barriers and works as follows:

- Define your problem as a question on a blank sheet of paper (For example, how can I break the service standards in my industry?)
- Write down and number all the possible solutions to this problem.
- If the problem is significant, the first 5 to 10 solutions you write down will be obvious, because they are generated spontaneously by the conscious mind.
- Solutions 10 to 15 will be difficult because they require hard thinking and force you to create new associations. Your initial instinct is to give up and name a solution you already wrote down as the ideal solution. Don't give in to this instinct and continue.
- Solutions 15 to 20 are tough to get. However, force yourself to continue until you have written 20 solutions on paper. Oftentimes, the breakthrough insights and the creative ideas will be found in the last 5 solutions.
- If you have used the 20 ways thinking technique, pick your best solution. Criteria could be ease of implementation, risk, cost or impact. Then, reformulate the solution into a new question (how can I...?). Perform another 20 ways exercise based on this question and you will be amazed by the quality of the new ideas.

Mindmapping

Next to idea generation, capturing and presenting ideas is essential in order to turn ideas into action. Take for example brainstorming. During a typical brainstorm, new ideas come at random and totally unorganized, especially when the subconscious mind is being accessed. To have an effective brainstorm, each idea has to be captured and written down first. Only then can ideas be evaluated and organized in lists, or bullet points, as a next step. A technique called "mindmapping" was pioneered by brain researcher Tony Buzan. Mindmapping uses a special way of writing down ideas to create new and better ideas by providing new relations and insights.

A typical mind map looks like a neurological pattern of the brain, where branches with ideas, observations and insights spring from a core idea in the middle of the paper. A mind map is often a colorful drawing with words, pictures, doodles and symbols that provide readers with a quick and memorable understanding of the issues. Extensive research has not only shown that mindmapping leads to more and better ideas, but also to a much deeper learning experience when used to learn complicated subjects.

Making a mind map is simple:

Act!

- Describe the subject in a few words in the middle of a blank page.
- Draw branches from the middle to the side of the page and name each branch with a word (or a drawing) describing ideas, concepts or associations linked to the main subject.
- Each branch can create a new branch with a new word. The branch expanding process is unlimited.
- After creating multiple branches, take a complete survey of all branches and find synergies and relationships between the words, ideas, concepts and drawings.
- When the mind map is finished you will notice that each time you review the picture, you will instantly remember the key concepts of the mind map.

- You will have different ideas when you use colored pens because the brain associates colors with certain concepts (such as blue with calm). These subconscious concepts trigger new associations and new ideas.

Cornell note taking

Memory is much less reliable than many people think. While the conscious part of your brain is excellent at reasoning, it is lousy at storing information. Most of us have learned the skill of note taking, writing down important points to review and remember at a later time.

Taking notes will therefore help increase the quality of your ideas tremendously.

One of the most effective methods for taking notes is the Cornell system. This is how it works:
- Divide a sheet of paper into three areas.
- Use the left part of the paper to write down the key words of the conversation.
- Use the right part to expand on the key words, with insights, ideas and actions.
- Use the bottom part to summarize the conversation afterwards, preferably within 24 hours.

This method not only makes your notes easily accessible and retrievable, but it also forces the brain to distill the essence of a conversation while listening.

The mastermind group

No success has ever been achieved in isolation. Innovating and breaking the standards requires support and advice from others.

This concept is called a "mastermind group," consisting of people outside your industry who are dedicated to your success.

No success has ever been achieved in isolation.

A small group of like-minded and ambitious people, the master-mind group, meets for mutual brainstorming and accountability sessions. Even the greatest of minds sometimes suffer from mental myopia. When you're stuck in your own thinking, you continue to breath your own mental exhaust fumes. The goal of a master-mind group is to provide fresh air to clear this thinking fog.

Here is how to implement a mastermind group:

- Create a group of a maximum of six of your peers who have seniority and level of experience similar to yours.
- Make sure there is chemistry between the members to facilitate spirited and open discussions.
- Meet at least once a month for two to three hours. Replace mastermind members who are absent frequently.
- Create an agenda for every meeting. Specify a topic for each member, and include discussion time.
- Don't let any one person dominate the conversation. Use the Native American talking stick method if necessary, where only the person holding a symbolic talking stick may speak. When this person is finished, the talking stick moves to the left.

- Assign accountabilities for progress and respect begin and end times.

Helping your mastermind members succeed will, in turn, help bolster your success by enhancing your personal creativity and innovativeness.

6

The power of strategic quitting

Business and career success is closely linked to the skill to free up energy and time while doing your current job or running your business. The time and energy release is essential to break through the hurdles and obstacles on your way to success. This chapter describes practical ways how to apply this high-performance principle that you have to let go in order to reach out.

The mindset of strategic quitting

While working with high-performance operations executives, we came across a most remarkable discovery: the most successful individuals were invariably very good at building processes and systems that took them almost completely out of the equation of their current job. One executive joked that she could do her job in two hours a week. She wasn't slothful. She had more than 2,000 people reporting to her, but she had built a system that took care of 95 percent of her responsibilities. She was involved only in key decisions and critical moments. This executive isn't unlike an airplane pilot, who is paid handsomely to perform flawlessly during only a fraction of the entire flight time (preparation, take off, emergencies and landing). By making herself obsolete, our high-performing executive used the freed-up time to stretch herself, sowing the seeds to smoothly transition to even bigger assignments.

The process of making yourself obsolete is called "strategic quitting." When I was a young boy, my father took me to a playground. The favorite equipment of many children there was the monkey bar: a set of horizontal bars, suspended in the air. Children cross the bars, hanging in the air while moving from bar to bar. When my father lifted me up and I was hanging there, I was simply unable to move. Then my father explained to me that you have to release one hand in order to move. In other words, you have to let go in order to reach out.

I never forgot this lesson: you have to make space first, before you can start doing new things. Doing more is no longer the answer to having too much to do. This mindset of strategic quitting is based on the idea that the less you do to achieve existing results, the more successful you will get new results.

The process of making yourself obsolete is called "strategic quitting."

Adopting the mindset of strategic quitting will help you to finally step out of the busy trap, become strategic with your own resources and focus on getting everything you can out of everything you have. It gives you a foundation to quickly move to high performance to accelerate your career, organization or business.

Stepping out of the hamster wheel to focus on marketing, innovation and strategy requires that you let go in order to reach out. There are only two ways to let go of activities: stop certain activities, or do less of certain activities.

How do you stop an activity or do less of an activity? These actions will help:

- **Delegation**: the ability to focus on talents and work together with others. This is the essence of high-performance teams: they seamlessly build on each other's strengths and thus compensate each other's weaknesses.
- **Elimination**: the ability to understand that the worst use of time isn't working inefficiently, but doing what shouldn't be done in the first place.
- **Outsourcing**: the ability to do only activities that are your highest and best use of time.
- **Systemization**: building processes and systems that reduce your personal involvement in your current job.

In this chapter we will take a detailed look at each of these four key behaviors.

Delegation

According to Albert Einstein, "everybody is a genius, but if you judge a fish by its ability to climb a tree, it will live its whole life believing it's stupid." This quote is a stark reminder that your job is to build on your strengths and not to correct your weaknesses. If you focus your entire life on compensating for weaknesses, you will end up with a large set of strong weaknesses. This is a recipe for mediocrity, not for success.

In order to spend your life building on your strengths, you must master the art of delegation. Delegation ensures that important work gets done by others, so you can focus your time and energy doing valuable things you love to do and consequently are very good at doing as well.

A common mistake is to think that delegation means giving your work to someone else. This isn't delegation, but management. Real delegation is something else. It means giving a task that is drudgery for you to someone who enjoys it. Real delegation paves the road to high performance in teams.

As an example, working with the software program SAP used to be a continuous exercise in frustration for me. However, I soon realized that I had a colleague who loved working with SAP, was very good at it and could do in two happy minutes what took me two dreadful hours. Our little delegation deal was quickly made. I gave her my SAP work and, in return, received a cool spreadsheet building task from her. This exchange gave me an opportunity to channel my inner engineering geek on a rainy Sunday afternoon. We were both happy, because we could employ our strengths.

Therefore, next time you run into difficult work, ask yourself who might love to do what you hate to do. The answer might surprise you, because no human brain is wired alike, resulting in very diverse work preferences. That is why people choose freely to become accountants, dentists or even engineers.

As a rule of thumb, remember the following: there are, generally speaking, only three things you do so well that they should never be done by someone else. Identify these three things and delegate the rest.

If you focus your entire life on compensating for weaknesses, you will end up with a large set of strong weaknesses.

Elimination

The worst use of your time isn't to do things inefficiently. The worst use of your time is to do things that shouldn't be done in the first place. Becoming excellent in irrelevant work prevents you from achieving high performance.

Many habits and activities were initiated in the past. They were useful at that time. Yet, even though the world has changed, people still continue to do the things that are no longer relevant to the modern world. For example, many organizations are in the business of producing reports. While these reports were useful in the past, they often no longer impact future success. Yet they are still being produced.

Here is a practical application: next time you need to write a routine report, write it, put it in a drawer and see what happens. If after four weeks, no one has expressed a need for it, this report is ready for elimination.

Zero-based thinking

Thinking is a high-energy, time-consuming activity. Therefore, humans naturally try to think in the shortest time possible and then return to their usual routines. As a result, you spend over 95 percent of your life operating on autopilot.

The same is true of your daily activities. You are a creature of habit and once a habit has been formed, you seldom think consciously about it again. However, many habits formed in the past might not be relevant today: because they no longer support your new goals, lifestyle or professional performance. Cutting back on these habit-related activities will free up vast amounts of energy that can be reinvested in more valuable activities.

You can actively steer this process of cutting back on non-supportive habits and activities by using the technique of zero-based thinking. In zero-based thinking ask yourself a brutal question: knowing what I know now, which of my current activities would I no longer initiate if I could start from the beginning?'

The answer to this question may be surprising. Next, commit to finding ways to reduce or even eliminate these habits and non-supportive activities. The resulting energy boost will be momentous and soon you will be brimming with creative ideas to fill the new space created in your life.

If you're running a strategy session in your company or organization, zero-based thinking can be applied with an activity called "Lights on, now what...?"

Here's how to set up this exercise:

Act!

- Imagine you just bought this company. You're part of the new management team and this is your first day in the office.
- Imagine you have no history and not a single constraint and ask yourself the following questions:
    - Which activities would I start immediately?
    - Which activities would I stop immediately?
    - Which activities would I do more of?
    - Which activities would I do less of?
- Define the most important activities and start moving rapidly toward your goal.

Vital few

Nature is unbalanced. In other words, input (effort) and output (results) aren't equally distributed. Therefore, the majority of results come from a minority of input activities. This phenomenon is known as the 80/20 rule or the vital few, and we see it everywhere. For example, 80 percent of taxes are being paid by 20 percent of people; 20 percent of your clothes are worn 80 percent of the time; 20 percent of your knowledge is used 80 percent of the time, etc.

Because the 80/20 rule is counter intuitive, many people are aware of it, but few actually use it consistently to simplify their lives and improve their conditions and results accordingly. Another reason the 80/20 approach is hardly used in organizations is due to the power of organizational entropy. Managers in large organizations often unconsciously tend to add complexity, because it poses interesting challenges and solidifies their organizational power base. Behavioral economists have noticed that once an organization has reached a threshold of about 1,000 employees, it no longer needs outside stimulus to keep itself busy.

The majority of results come from a minority of input activities.

The 80/20 rule is a natural law that acts similar to other natural laws such as gravity. While you may resist the resulting inequality as unfair, at the end of the day nature prevails. High-performance individuals, therefore, understand the importance of learning to use this law to achieve their goals before they attempt to fight it.

Here are ways you can immediately begin to use the 80/20 rule to simplify your life and business and rapidly improve results:

- At the beginning of every year, go through your client list and let go of the bottom 20 percent. (Suggestion: introduce them to your competition.) These clients typically cause you the most headaches and give you the least amount of results.
- Double your management attention for the top 20 percent of your clients. They usually produce the bulk of your results and are a pleasure the work with.

- Cut your information intake: 80 percent of the information you receive is noise anyway, while only 20 percent is typically relevant to your life and goals. To distinguish between noise and relevant information, keep in mind the following: if information doesn't trigger you to take action, it won't help you move toward your goals and is therefore, by definition, noise. Don't confuse busy-ness with achievement.

- When it comes to high performance, doing more is no longer the answer to too much to do. Instead, the answer is to focus on the vital few.

Triage

"The magistrate does not consider trifles," so says ancient Roman law. Being conscious of time isn't a modern phenomenon. All of us do good work. However, the difference between mediocre results and wild success is whether you're working merely on useful things, or on what gives you the biggest bang for the buck in return. Triage is a quick priority setting technique that can create the difference between running on autopilot and achieving dramatic results. Triage is based on the risk-reward ratio on the one hand and three easy criteria on the other. It enables individuals and organizations to shift focus to activities that really matter and overcome the setbacks of classic priority setting.

The problem with classic priority setting

You will get the best business outcome and professional performance if you conserve energy and work only on targeted activities with a low risk and a high reward. Classic priority setting usually considers only two main variables or variations thereof: impact (size of the opportunity) and probability of success (a percentage in which the risk factor is taken into account). Often, priority decisions are based on the product of these two variables.

The expression of risk as a percentage of success leads to inaccurate conclusions. For instance, while winning a lottery has an enormous impact, the probability of success is so small that any strategy of getting rich through lottery participation is doomed to fail. In other words, high-risk, high-reward activities must be avoided. The fact that we have lottery winners isn't an excuse for having lotteries.

This analysis leads us to four areas of operational activity:

- **Area I**: Low risk, low reward. This is small thinking. Operating in this quadrant is a complete waste of time. Get out ASAP.
- **Area II**: High risk, low reward. Exit now. Activities in this quadrant should be stopped immediately.
- **Area III**: High risk, high reward. Here will be dragons. Move cautiously, carefully balancing every decision and keeping your eyes on the prize. Better yet, find other activities.
- **Area IV**: Low risk, high reward. This is what we call the turkey shoot. Move quickly and aggressively, even when only 80 percent ready. The fruits are ready to harvest and the risks are small.

Classic priority setting doesn't make risk and reward transparent. As a result professionals often find themselves focusing energy in area I where the probability of success is high, thus activities look attractive. However, we end up working on trivial and inconsequential activities. For example, this is true for most cost cutting activities

Opposite of low risk, low reward, classic priority setting often leads to working on 'high risk, high reward' activities as well (area III): the lure of high impact makes these activities attractive. However, odds of success are low and energy should be spent on other activities.

You will get the best business outcome and professional performance if you conserve energy and work only on targeted activities with a low risk and a high reward.

What is triage?

Triage takes a different approach than classic priority setting and is based on two essential rules:

- **Rule number 1**: No activities other than area IV activities (low risk, high reward) will be considered. Be brutal and refuse to work on anything else.
- **Rule number 2**: Priorities for low risk, high-reward activities are set based on seriousness, urgency and growth.

- *Seriousness*: the business impact of the activity, which can range from minor benefits to complete business transformation.
- *Urgency*: the window of opportunity. A looming short-term deadline will, for instance, create a high urgency.
- *Growth*: what the impact of the activity will look like in the future if nothing is done. For instance, if an opportunity naturally grows smaller in time, the growth score will be lower as well.

Why triage will accelerate business outcomes

Triage accelerates positive business outcomes, because it forces an organization to work only on activities that create the biggest positive impact. Triage answers the most important question in time management: what is the best use of my time right now? These are area IV activities.

Furthermore, triage creates the total picture of all activities. It steers our energy to thinking bigger and searching for better initiatives, instead of lazily embracing the usual suspects and trying to make mediocre initiatives work.

Finally, triage helps to elegantly dismiss any activity that looks like good work, but in reality is either a waste of time or not worth the risk.

Act! *Here are some additional practical tips and tricks to achieve more with triage:*

- Triage can be applied equally to priority setting and problem solving. Keep in mind that problem solving leads to restoring the original situation, while priority setting focuses on opportunities and therefore on higher performance.
- If there are no low risk, high reward activities to consider,

spend more time and energy on getting new ideas. If this fails too, you may need to rethink the question of what success looks like and why you want success in the first place. Other goals might be more suitable. For instance, if you have failed to capture a certain market niche, you may try your luck at another market niche. In this case, business success might still be within reach.

- Once you have identified your priorities, take massive action on a maximum of three priorities. Get in motion: risks are low and speed is often paramount. As the acclaimed management thinker Peter Drucker observed, effective executives have only one or two key initiatives in mind. On these key initiatives they move with blinding speed. Remaining effort is delegated, postponed or eliminated.
- Time-box a maximum of three major low-risk, high-reward activities and organize massive action around the start fast, finish strong principle.
- Perform executive triage every six months on your complete organizational and personal activity list. Get rid of at least 10 percent of your activities and use the extra energy to make a bigger impact on your major activities.
- Promote high risk, high reward to low risk, high-reward activities by creatively looking for and implementing different ideas to mitigate risk. For instance, getting additional insurance against devastating business losses can seriously reduce the risk profile of many activities and make these activities suddenly very attractive.

Not to do list
The enemy of ultimate perseverance is distraction. If you could focus your mind on a single goal for a long period of time, the results

would be staggering. Unfortunately, the brain isn't naturally wired to shut out distractions and move ahead with a single task. If 25 years of practice to become a serene, single-minded and accomplished Zen master sounds too much work, the good news is that there are other simpler ways to help you achieve perseverance.

- When you feel the urge to do something new but realize this activity won't help you achieve your goals, write it down on a not-to-do list. Writing it down brings your brain into executive mode, which helps you let go of the thought so it will no longer distract you.

- Create a someday/maybe list. If the urge to do something new has merit but should not be done now or in the near future, put it on a someday/maybe list. You can then review this list of activities and ideas on a regular basis. This list helps you remember your good ideas, put them in a trusted place and, most importantly, get them out of your head.

- Create a never-do-to-make-a-living list. This is a list containing projects, activities or initiatives that might help you achieve your goals but isn't the type of work you like to do. This list is a great tool to make quick, concise and consistent decisions. For instance, you may detest ghost writing. If ghost writing is on your never-do-to-make-a-living list, every time someone dangles a ghost writing opportunity in front of you, you can decline with a smile and without second thoughts. High on my never-do-to-make-a-living list is cold calling, or, approaching strangers by telephone hoping to create a business relationship. The activity of cold calling would make me miserable, even if it could somehow help me tremendously to achieve my goals.

Which one of these three lists would make you unstoppable?

The enemy of ultimate perseverance is distraction.

Outsourcing

We outsource all the time. We buy cookies at the supermarket, have our hair cut by a stylist and obtain software designed by a team of professionals. Outsourcing is natural to us, yet it is a behavior that isn't always natural in business. How many times have you seen executives buy office supplies, managers use their precious time setting up new software or engineers mindlessly busy adding rows of data in a spreadsheet?

The most important reason outsourcing is an absolute must to achieve Preeminence is opportunity cost. The time spent going out and buying your own lunch could have been spent on marketing, innovation and strategy. You might have saved some money getting your own lunch, yet the savings are probably insignificant compared to the opportunities you could have gained by doing the most important things for your business. You will, therefore, rapidly become Preeminent if you focus your time and energy on the few things that positively impact your business. Simply outsource all else.

Systemization

You will get only predictable and sustainable results by projects or processes. A project is a systematic approach toward achieving a clearly defined goal. A process is a set of defined steps that continue to give predictable results. Often, the result of a project is the design of a process. Take, for example, a project to optimize invoice payment.

You will get only predictable and sustainable results by projects or processes.

Your aim should be to systemize as much as possible in your business. Here is why:

- Building processes gives controllable results. If you don't have a process for selling, you will be at the mercy of someone else's process for buying. And this is seldom to your advantage.
- As described in chapter 2, creating processes will enable you to shift time and energy from working in to working on your business, thus enabling you to achieve Preeminence.
- Using processes gives you predictable results, which are the hallmark of a Preeminent business. Your ideal should be to predict your cash flow six months from now based on the activities you engage in today.

A focus on systemization is important to accelerate your career. The best career advice ever given to me was to become outstanding in my job and make myself indispensable. You should become so essential in the eyes of your boss, organization and clients that the thought of lose you will create distress throughout the organization.

It was also the worst career advice ever given to me. Here's why. The skills required to become the absolute best and indispensable in your current job, often obstruct the skills needed to expand, move out of your comfort zone and take giant steps toward your next job. In other words, what has got you here will no longer get you there. For instance, because you often can't rely on your existing support group to help you get a new and better job, you need to build a new support group. Doing so requires a different use of your time and energy.

The best way to rapidly advance your career or your business is, therefore, counterintuitive: focus your energy on finding ways to ensure that your presence is less and less required to do the job you were hired to do. This lessening of your job's dependence on you defines the difference between working in your job and working on your job. The less you do, the more successful you will be. For example, if you're an engineer responsible for troubleshooting at a chemical plant, look for ways to automate and systemize this process. If you do this, three very interesting things will happen:

- Automation and systemization can often easily be copied to other parts of the company. By innovating a new approach, instead of supporting one plant, all of a sudden you will add more value by helping multiple plants at the same time.
- You will free up time and energy, which can then be focused on doing other activities. These activities may not be part of

your current job, but can nevertheless be more valuable to the organization.

- You will gain skills and experience essential to prepare yourself to move to your next job. For example, driving an automation project to other parts of the organization will help you gain experience as a project leader and a manager.

High performance starts with a shift in thinking. Instead of spending your time and energy to improve your performance in your current job, turn your focus to find ways to make your current job obsolete. You know that you've succeeded when you have taken yourself out of the job equation. The litmus test is that no one will be needed to fill your position when you move to a different job.

7

Increase performance, not potential

Imagine you own an old computer and its speed is limited by the amount of random access memory, or RAM. If you were to replace this computer's processor, you would increase its potential: you have increased the possibility that it will be faster in the future. However, if you increase its RAM, you have improved performance. The effects and benefits of this action are immediate.

The distinction between increasing performance versus potential is very important if you rapidly want to move to high performance. A big trap in business is that significant energy, time and money are often spent on what could be, instead of immediate nourishment.

Typical examples of choosing potential over performance:
- The decision to invest in future capacity. The thinking is that if you invest in it, the results will follow. They seldom do.
- Training of people in skills they might need for the future. Newly acquired skills will be effective only if they can be applied immediately and consistently. Otherwise, training is a waste of time, money and energy.
- Intake of information that is not immediately actionable. When was the last time you spent an hour browsing magazines without getting a new single actionable idea?

High performance is therefore not the same as high potential. In this chapter we will discuss a few pragmatic elements to immediately improve performance.

Theory of constraints

Between yourself and your ambitious goals lies one major constraint. This obstacle is your bottleneck, or your rock. The higher your goals, the bigger this rock.

The rock hinders the speed at which you achieve your goal. Your focus should be to identify and prepare to overcome this constraint. For example, to have more impact on your organization, your biggest rock could be your lack of experience in giving convincing presentations. A focus on improving presentation skills will, therefore, help you get where you want in the fastest way possible.

How do you find your key constraints for Preeminence? Ask your- **Act!**
self the following questions:

- *Which one skill, if I had it right here, right now, would have the greatest positive impact on my business or professional performance?*
- *If I would hire myself as a consultant for my own business, what would be the first thing I would recommend to change?*
- *What must I do in an excellent way to achieve my high future goals?*

Then start overcoming your key constraint. See yourself as a work in progress: attach skill development to goal achieving. Once you start to develop the necessary skills, you'll see yourself moving rapidly toward achieving your goals.

After you have solved your key constraint, a new key constraint may pop up. Continue to use this process to identify and overcome future hurdles.

Decision making

Another essential part of improving performance is decision making. Decision making is an essential action for any professional and leader. Decision comes from the Latin root de-cedere, which translates to slicing or cutting away. A decision, therefore, involves committing without a safety line to buffer your doubts. The power of commitment is therefore an enormous force. If wielded correctly, this power will help you move quickly toward high performance.

Decision making is a habit, The more decisions you make consciously, the easier it will be to commit and move ahead more forcefully. The quality of your decision making habit is determined both by the frequency of decision making and the quality of the decisions. So, how can you improve your decision making habit and make high quality and high performance decisions?

Rational versus emotional

Humans are nearly 100% emotional. In other words, virtually every decision you make is subconscious, after which you engage your conscious mind to rationalize your decisions. To improve the quality of your decision making, you must therefore feed your subconscious mind with information and data, which requires accurate thinking about all decisions.

These three elements will help you improve decision making:
- Objectives versus alternatives
- Musts versus wants
- Risks versus rewards

Objectives versus alternatives

A simple way to improve your decision making skills is to distinguish between objectives (the inn at the end of the journey) and alternatives (the different paths to get to the inn). The easiest way to make better decisions is to develop alternatives first. For example, if your objective is to grow your business, you can put an advertisement in the local newspaper (=marketing), develop a new service (=innovation) or explore an alliance with another company (=strategy).

Musts versus wants

A must is an objective that has to be met, regardless of the decision. A want is an objective that would be a nice bonus to achieve, but is not critical. For instance, during a search for a suitable manufacturing plant location, a must could be access to critical utilities such as electricity and a want is close access to shipping, because access to a harbor would be nice, but there are other ways to transport your goods.

Risks versus rewards

An easy way to address risk versus reward is to scale risk from -10 (=apocalyptic) to -1 (small nuisance) and scale reward from 1 (some local benefit) to 10 (massive global breakthrough). A good decision is always low on the risk scale and high on the reward scale. Never the other way around.

These three elements all play a role in making quality decisions. The more thought you give to these elements, the better the decisions you will make.

Decision making for leaders

As a business leader, decisions can be made by you, your team, or both. In the context of your work, there are five ways to make decisions:

- **Imperial**. You simply decide and inform others
- **Consult individually**. You ask people for their input individually, then you decide yourself.
- **Consult as group**. You ask the group for collective input, then you decide.
- **Democracy**: you engage the group and let the majority decide.
- **Delegated**: you let the team decide.

Every situation requires an evaluation of which decision making style would make most sense. For example, for planning the office party, a team decision might be appropriate. However, in case of the Titanic hitting the iceberg, a dictatorial style should be your default position.

Project management: good, cheap, fast

The only way to achieve lasting and predictable results is either by doing projects, such as getting a new key client, or by building systems, such as implementing a new referral system. Interestingly enough, the process of doing projects or building systems adheres to certain laws. These laws are unbreakable (to the chagrin of many project managers). A perfect example is the law of project sacrifice, also known as "good, cheap, fast." Pick two.

The law of project sacrifice dictates that whenever you do a project or build a system, you can achieve only two goals simultaneously, while consciously sacrificing one other goal to make this happen. This practice means that a project can be:

- Good and cheap. But never fast. Think of building your own garden shed.
- Good and fast. But never cheap. Take, for example, outsourcing your taxes to a tax professional.
- Cheap and fast. But never good. When was the last time you used duct tape to temporarily fix something?

A perfect example is the law of project sacrifice, also known as "good, cheap, fast." Pick two.

Always decide beforehand which of these three goals is the least painful for you to sacrifice. Then bite the bullet and focus on achieving the other two objectives. The biggest mistake project managers make is to avoid making this decision upfront. If you fail to sacrifice a goal, your project will end up lousy, expensive and way over time.

Here are some practical applications of the law of project sacrifice.

Act!

- If it is not possible to sacrifice either good, cheap or fast, avoid the project all together. The project will never achieve its intended outcome and your energy and time is better used somewhere else.
- If you make the sacrifice, leverage your decision to the maximum. For instance, speed to market (fast) will often offset the fact you can't complete the project cheaply.
- Real artist's ship. To make a difference, you have to produce something. Unfortunately, many people fall in love with perfection and suddenly, in their minds, good equals flawless. This thinking leads to paralysis and an inability to get things done. A better way of thinking about your next project is therefore "good enough, reasonably cheap, blindingly fast. Pick two."

Magnificent projects require courage. And courage starts by making the decision to let go in order to reach out.

Overcoming procrastination
The part of your brain called the lizard hates risk and uncertainty and will therefore fight change (which naturally includes risk and uncertainty) tooth and nail. This struggle leads to procrasti-

nation. Procrastination is defined as knowing that you need to do something, while not doing it and feeling miserable about it.

There is, however, a way to prevent the lizard brain from getting upset while thinking through a project. It is called the natural planning model and it comprises these five steps that, if executed in this sequence, provide a natural thinking flow:

1. Define the vision and mission. Imagine wild success.
2. Define the guiding principles of the journey to get there. Guiding principles are the boundary conditions for the successful journey.
3. Get all ideas out through brainstorming. Plaster the walls with all the weird, crazy and sometimes good ideas that can help you achieve success. A good brainstorm aims for volume, not quality: it takes 1,000 bad ideas to get one good idea.
4. Organize the ideas into a plan with follow-up actions.
5. Execute the plan.

Serendipity

Good things happen to people who are in motion. Whenever one door closes, another door opens somewhere else. This state of constant movement and opportunity is called serendipity, which explains why successful people seem to attract even more success.

Serendipity is triggered by clear goals and constant motion. It is connected to the workings of the Reticular Activating System (RAS). When an organization knows exactly what it wants to achieve and constantly takes steps to move in the right direction, serendipitous events will happen. Or, more bluntly, motion beats meditation every time.

You can use the idea of smallest achievable perfection (SMAP) to force yourself to progress toward your goals. A SMAP is a small step that is perfected. For instance, to build the skill of effective public speaking, a SMAP can be to focus on making eye contact with the audience. Once you have done this, go to the next SMAP, such as projecting your voice to the end of the room.

Motion beats meditation every time.

21-day habit

Habits have an enormous impact on the quality of life. It takes 21 days to form the beginnings of a new habit, which is a neurological pathway in our brain between place A and place B. Once this pathway is created, following that pathway becomes easier with every use. Therefore, repetition is the key to forming habits.

Here is the trick to create your own brain pathways and build new habits: pick one habit at a time, act consistently and consciously on this habit every day, don't waiver and don't give in for 21 days. After 21 days you will have created the beginning of a new pathway in your brain.

After that, it will take decreasingly less effort to follow through on your new habit. The new habit becomes increasingly easier and will in the end become second nature to you, reinforced with every use.

8

Communicate anything to anyone

Edward Howard Armstrong was a brilliant engineer who single-handedly invented FM radio technology. To most of us, however, his massive contribution to science and engineering is unknown. He combined absolute brilliance with a rough and difficult personality, which made him simply unable to win powerful people over to help him implement his ideas.

Though his inventions continue to live on, the name Edward Howard Armstrong remains a small footnote in the history of science.

Comparing and contrasting his life with people like Henry Ford, Nicola Tesla and Thomas Edison, it's clear that, while having a similar scientific brilliance to Armstrong, these great men had the ability to persuade powerful people to support their causes.

The ability to communicate ideas effectively to key decision makers is a business skill critical to achieve success in the easiest way possible.

The ability to communicate ideas effectively to key decision makers is a business skill critical to achieve success in the easiest way possible.

CLEAR communication

Your communication, such as email, competes with Facebook, the Stock Market, newspaper headlines, billboards on the road and the latest Twitter. Tough competition. If you want to be heard, make sure you bypass the mental filters of the receiver. Make sure your communication is crisp and relevant. An excellent technique is Bill Jensen's CLEAR model:

- **C̲ontext**: why this communication is important to what your audience is currently doing.
- **L̲ist of resources required**: money, people, time.
- **E̲xpectations**: what wild success looks like.
- **A̲ctivities**: all actions needed for success.
- **R̲eturn**: how the message benefits your audience.

Learning styles

How can the same speech get standing ovations by one raving crowd, yet invoke only polite applause when delivered to a different group? It could be that you simply fail to address each of the four essential questions that make a magnificent speech. Let me explain.

Your brain is a goal-seeking machine. Because of the sensory bombardment assaulting you every second, the mind operates with specific filters. These filters determine whether new information is relevant or can be dismissed. To communicate new information effectively to others, you have to find a way to bypass these filters. How do you do so?

You absorb information using one of four information transfer mechanisms. These mechanisms are called learning styles and take the form of critical questions in the conscious mind. The questions must be answered to make new information relevant. Understanding these learning styles is especially important to communicate new ideas effectively to larger audiences in presentations, training sessions and workshops.

If, for instance, you happen to speak about the power of visualization, each audience member will have one of the following four questions floating in their minds:

- *How is this information relevant to me?* This philosopher's learning style covers 35 percent of your listeners in a typical audience. You can reach the philosophers by quickly connecting to the "what's in it for me?" question. For example, if you understand the power of visualization, you'll achieve your goals much easier.

- *What is the principle behind this idea?* This scientist's learning style covers 20 percent of your listeners. You can reach the scientist types by explaining the process and methodology behind the new idea. Use logic to make your point. For example, you could explain that visualization is effective, because it triggers the subconscious mind to become aware of people, ideas and circumstances that can help you achieve your goal.

- *What steps are required for this idea?* This engineer's learning style includes 20 percent of your listeners. You can reach the engineers by communicating a recipe with practical steps to apply the idea. Providing a checklist is very effective. For example, you could explain the sequential steps to effectively using visualization.

- *How can I use this idea to improve my life?* This entrepreneur's learning style includes 25 percent of the listeners. You can reach the entrepreneurs by applying the new idea to solve an actual problem. For example, an audience exercise using visualization to find creative ways to increase revenue in a business would be great for appealing to this audience.

You'll reach everyone in the audience only when you answer all four questions. For maximum impact, answer these questions in the sequence listed.

The power of know-feel-do

Some time ago I was asked whether I do motivational speeches. I answered that being motivational is the minimum requirement for any speaker. What really matters, however, is how the audience will be better off after I'm gone.

Your job as a presenter is to improve the condition of the audience. All else is just commentary.

A great presentation is therefore never about you, your ideas or your company. Instead, a great presentation is about the people listening to you.

If you really want to present with impact, start your preparation with this one magic question: "how will the audience be better off once I have left the room?"

Then design your talk using the power of know-feel-do:
- This is what I want the audience to know.
- This is how I want the audience to feel.
- This is what I want the audience to do.

If you ignore these objectives, you become just an empty entertainer or a droning bore. Both are equally bad.

Motivation is overrated. It is the conversation afterwards that counts.

Communication styles

Human beings are interesting creatures. They're all wired differently and therefore have very different preferences, ideas and natural inclinations. This variety is true for communication styles as well. You may have the best ideas in the world, but if you are unable to communicate effectively, nothing happens. It is a mistake to assume that your communication partner has the same communication style you have. This mistake can be fatal to any important initiative or idea.

Here's a useful approach to deal with different communication styles and convince others of your ideas. Communication preferences can be plotted along two different axes:

- Task-oriented versus people-oriented;
- Asking style versus telling style.

Using these two axes, you can identify four different communication styles:

- **Task and ask**. These people are analytics. The typical language they use is "I think." They use logic to determine what they want. If you want to persuade an analytic, focus on the quality of your service and support.
- **Task and tell**. These are drivers. You will often hear "I will." They know what they want and like to be in control. Therefore, always provide drivers with options to choose from.
- **People and ask**. We call these people amiable. For them, it is essential to build and keep relationships and they often use "I feel" in their conversations. Performance guarantees are essential to persuade an amiable.
- **People and tell**. These are relators, who typically use the language of "I want." They like to be in the spotlight and can be persuaded by endorsements, referrals and testimonials from people they respect.

Remember that your communication style will differ from the style of your communication partner most of the time. Therefore, if you get stuck, don't try to persuade others by using more of what you are already doing. Instead, use the language and sensitivities of other communication styles to persuade others of your viewpoint. For example, if you're an analytic, don't use more data as you normally would. As an alternative, add options, guarantees and referrals to the mix.

If you use this approach consistently, you will be surprised how smoothly you are able to communicate anything with anyone.

Open with impact

How do you start a presentation? Suggested ideas are quotes, interesting statistics or stories. Each of these strategies will create interest, but only if they are part of a great opening. A great opening takes a maximum of two minutes and covers five areas:

- **Attention**. Use silence, look around the room and smile to draw people in.
- **Information**. Tell them up front what the talk will be about, instead of revealing your purpose somewhere along the way. Suspense is excellent for Hollywood movies. It falls flat with a presentation.
- **Expectation**. Explain how they can apply the information afterward. This is the distinction between potential (knowing how you might use the information somewhere in the future) and performance (knowing how you can use the information immediately).
- **Engagement**. Tell them how the information is important to them. It creates the distinction between a general talk and something of immediate interest to each audience member. It answers the most important question: What's in it for me?
- **Involvement**. Involve them as a player, not a spectator. The best openings invite people to participate immediately by, for example, asking them to raise their hands to answer questions or offer ideas.

Executive communication

The ability to influence executives and other decision makers is essential to achieve your goals. Effective and persuasive communication to executives starts with understanding three key mindsets:

- You will have no problem getting what you want in life if you give others what they want. In other words, you can be successful only if you help others become successful first. Life is more like a Chinese take-away than a restaurant. In a restaurant you eat first and pay afterward. At a Chinese take-away you pay before you eat. In other words, you have to give first to improve the life of others in order to receive.

- The objective of your communication is not to pitch your ideas, dazzle everyone with your brilliance or be adored by a cheering crowd. Instead, your goal should be to show decision makes how your ideas can contribute to their success.

- In order to be heard, you have to be remarkable. You are competing for attention and your adversaries are hundreds of emails per day, the latest corporate crisis and plunging stock markets. The attention span of a goldfish is five seconds, and that of any corporate executive or a potential client is not much better. You, therefore, must stand out and be remarkable in the few moments that you get the decision maker's attention.

These three mindsets give you the guiding principles to assemble the nuts and bolts of an effective communication strategy.

Time

Now that you have successfully identified the necessary mindsets, it's time to focus on your biggest challenge: time. The most important number in our life (and for that matter in any executive's life) is 1,440 – the number of minutes in one day. The good news is that every day starts with a new batch of 1,440 minutes. The bad news is that the number of minutes in a day is fixed: nothing will change this. Effective communication requires us, therefore, to be conscious of other people's time.

With effective use of time as your guiding principle, take a look at two typical situations you might face: what to do when you have 30 seconds and what to do when you have 20 minutes?

30 seconds: the elevator pitch

The term elevator pitch was coined to describe a situation when a cash-starved inventor entered an elevator together with an important investment banker. How does he take advantage of this 30-second window of opportunity?

Realize there are three questions floating in the investment banker's head:
- Who are you?
- What do you do?
- Why does that matter to me?

Answering these three questions can be daunting, but doable if you prepare well. Failure to answer all of these questions within 30 seconds will make your elevator pitch fall flat.

20 minutes: the executive presentation

You have been asked to present your groundbreaking idea to the executive committee. A powerful strategy to pass this challenge successfully is to use the rules of 30-20-10-1.

These rules are as follows:
- **Rule of 30**. Most likely you will use slides. This rule dictates that the minimum font size in your slides should be 30. (This

font size is derived by dividing the age of the oldest partici-
pant in your audience by two. With 60-year-old executives in
your audience, your minimum font size should therefore be
30.) When text in your slides is BIG you are forced to use few
words to communicate the essentials.

- **Rule of 20**. You should use a maximum of 20 minutes to pitch
your idea. After this time you will undoubtedly be brutally interrupted and lose control of your presentation, which isn't
necessarily a big problem if you have communicated your
main points in the first 20 minutes.
- **Rule of 10**. Your total presentation should be a maximum of
10 slides, with additional slides allocated to the appendix.
- **Rule of 1**. This rule covers the most important slide in your
10-slide deck, the executive summary, which contains what
you want your audience to know, feel and do

The perfect pitch

Logic makes people think and emotion makes people act. That's
why many decisions are made on a gut feeling and the logic behind
the decision is a storyline, often crafted with care and beauty afterward. For example, many consultants are hired to write strategic reports after strategic decisions have already been taken.

Too often logic is compared to physical exercise: the more you
do it, the better you get. This belief has led to many exhaustive
meetings, where the next round of a gazillion additional slides is
used to beat the audience into submission. As you've seen earlier,
less is more would make our meetings and work more effective.

With a surplus of verbosity all around, you have an opportunity to shine: a brief, persuasive proposal will make you stand out
in any crowd. So, how do you craft brevity in a proposal without
creating holes in your logic?

There are six key elements to make any proposal attractive, brief and logically sound. This knowledge can be applied immediately and will give a stellar boost to your chances of quick and decisive approvals.

Logic makes people think and emotion makes people act.

Six building blocks of a great proposal
A great proposal covers six key building blocks. The first two blocks focus on the problem, the next four focus on the solution

Building block 1: What is the problem? Everyone can agree on the definition of a problem. However, it would be a mistake to settle for one definition quickly, consequently leaving out a host of possible creative solutions. Therefore, define the problem in at least three different ways. For instance, "our EBIT is 10 percent below forecast," "our customers buy 20 percent less volume," and "our production cost is 25 percent higher than anticipated."

Building block 2: The problem is significant. It's important not to waste time and energy solving problems that are insignificant to begin with. Don't fall into that trap and make a clear connection with the critical business objectives. An example of a significant problem could be "our low EBIT will leave us cash strapped and will jeopardize the launch of our new product. This new product is essential to meet our future growth targets."

Building block 3: What is the solution? The more problem definitions, the more powerful the solutions become. Here are some examples of powerful solutions:

- We can update the forecast to reflect our new business reality and adapt EBIT targets.
- We can train our staff to improve sales skills.
- We can cut production cost by shutting down idle assets.
- Pick your best solution. In this example, your hypothetical solution is to improve your sales skills.

Building block 4: The solution is feasible. The key question to determine feasibility is: has it been done before? If so, will you still stay within your organizational, ethical and legal boundaries if you apply this solution too? Too often, proposals take a pleasant stroll in fantasyland instead of taking a cold, hard look at reality. Omnipresent statements like "we have no other choice" and "we are awesome at innovation, so we'll pull off this communication strategy easily," as well as overestimating irrelevant and perceived strong organizational skills should be avoided. Instead, build your arguments within realistic margins. For example, sales skills training is an ideal solution, because it is widely available, can be implemented quickly and has a proven record of success.

Building block 5: The solution is effective. To be successful, your best solution must be a direct fix to the business problem. For instance, additional sales skills will bring in more revenue to compensate for the higher production cost and bolster EBIT. Be bold in proposing an effective solution. Don't waste time on half-hearted solutions. Teaching cannibals how to eat with knife and fork is hardly progress.

Building block 6: The advantages of the solution outweigh the disadvantages. Each solution has disadvantages. Make a list of at least five disadvantages. Be honest and brutal. In the end, don't give decision makers too much opportunity to step into a gloom and doom mindset by forcing them to generate the negatives themselves. Also, list additional advantages to your solution. These advantages can be tangible (such as "sales skills will lead to cross selling, which can boost revenue further") and intangible ("increased sales skills mean better retention of key people").

Rebutting proposals

If your aim is to counter proposals effectively, a template for making good proposals will be extremely helpful. A proposal is only as good as its weakest link. If one of the six key proposal building blocks is weak or missing, the entire proposal is weak. Therefore, apply laser-like focus to any proposal and home in exclusively on the weakest part. As an example, to rebut a glorious proposal about the stunning effects of introducing a company-wide team-building program, focus on the effectiveness of the proposal. Imagine this company doesn't have teams (groups with shared objectives), but committees (groups with individual objectives). The rebuttal to the proposal then becomes: "you simply cannot team-build a committee."

Practical tips and tricks to make any proposal shine

Act!

Here is some additional advice for consistently creating winning proposals.

- **There's no silver bullet**. Business proposals are seldom scientific. For every supporting argument, any creative mind can generate at least three counterarguments. Therefore, avoid the temptation to base a proposal on only one argument. Throw a wide net and use a set of powerful arguments to support your claim.
- **Statement, logic, example**. A powerful technique to give body to your proposal is to follow each statement by logic and then by an example. Doing so will solidify the building blocks of your proposal and make it harder for your opponents to put a monkey wrench in your well-crafted logic. Here is an example of the statement/logic/example format: Sales skills can be improved (statement). Sales is a skill. Each top salesperson has started at the bottom and moved upward only because of skill building and application (logic). After a one-week sales training, revenues at company XYZ went up by 11 percent in the first three months (example).

Don't waste time on half-hearted solutions. Teaching cannibals how to eat with a knife and fork, is hardly progress.

Feed forward

To help people improve, you usually give feedback. You observe the behavior of others, and afterward tell them what went wrong and what could be improved. To take the sharp edges off, you often use a salami tactic, hiding the constructive criticism between several layers of positive observations. This framework is often used in performance reviews.

The problem, however, is that negative feedback triggers our lizard brain: the part that fears change and interprets criticism as a risk of being cast out of the comfortable environment of the tribe. When the lizard brain kicks in, our neo-cortex (thinking brain) shuts down, making it impossible to positively absorb feedback. Therefore, feedback becomes ineffective and no improvement is achieved.

You can circumvent your lizard brain by using the process of feed forward developed by the renowned coach Marshall Goldsmith. In feed forward you simply share your best ideas for improvement with others, without referring to an observed behavior. This practice dramatically increases the chance of good ideas being absorbed.

Feed forward is a powerful technique, especially for sharing ideas between people in larger groups. Here's how it works:

1. Define the area where the group would like to improve (for example, how to spend less time on email).
2. Split the group and team up in pairs. The first person shares his or her best idea with the second person (such as learn to type 50 words per minute).
3. The second person only listens and gives positive feedback at the end (such as "thank you for sharing this idea.") No criticism or judgment is allowed.

4. Reverse roles and let the second person share his or her best idea. (such as to check email only twice a day).
5. After sharing, the listener gives a summary and some positive feedback (like "thank you for giving me this idea.")
6. The pair splits up and each person finds a new partner to repeat the feed-forward process with.

After the group has applied this feed-forward process repeatedly, each person will have received multiple ideas for improvement. Some of these ideas will be actionable, which will trigger an improvement loop.

9

The incredible time machine

The eminent physicist John Wheeler once said that time is nature's way of ensuring everything doesn't happen all at once. Contrary to what many believe, you cannot manage time: no amount of willpower or effort can reverse, stop or accelerate time. All we can manage is how we use our time.

Most of us have significant room for improvement in this area. In business and professional life, you exchange time (spent in mental or physical labor) for money. The results of this bargain are shockingly poor. By age 50, the average working citizen in advanced economies has accumulated $100,000 in wealth, which translates to average savings of $2 per working hour. Not a good deal.

Improving on this statistic requires a radical new approach to how to use time. This approach goes beyond the mechanics of time management. You often understand good time management habits, yet applying those habits consistently takes a conscious decision, very deliberate effort and especially a defined mindset.

These approaches and habits typically result in doing ten, a hundred or even a thousand times more than the average professional and business owner.

A study of high-performance people reveals that they have specific mindsets and habits when it comes to use of time. These approaches and habits typically result in doing ten, a hundred or even a thousand times more than the average professional and business owner. (And no, this extra work doesn't necessarily translate into 80-hour work weeks.) Watching these people in action is like entering an incredible time machine, getting things done seemingly without too much effort.

The good news is that you can build your own incredible time machine to achieve your goals in the easiest, fastest and most elegant way possible. In this chapter you'll explore the mindsets of these high-performing individuals, as well as a blueprint of the 13 most effective habits for time mastery.

These mindsets and habits, if embraced and applied consistently, have the potential to move you at warp speed from where you are to where you want to be.

The mindset

Time is the great equalizer. No matter the circumstances, every day starts with the same amount of time: 1,440 minutes. To be as effective and efficient as possible, you must consciously use your allocated time. Every minute counts. The difference between good use and best use of your time means the difference between average performance and stunning results.

Highest and best use of your time

The concept of highest and best use of time is a key principle for high performance. All your activities have three different dimensions:

- Your competence level to do the task.
- Your passion to be engaged with the task

- The value the task brings to others.

With these three dimensions in mind, you can take a systematic look at your activities to find your highest and best use of time.

- If you are competent, passionate, yet you don't create value to others, you have a hobby.
- If you are passionate, create value for others but aren't competent, you are a well-meaning amateur.
- If you create value for others, are competent but lack passion, you have a nine-to-five job.

You can therefore become excellent at using your time only with activities that meet all three criteria: you are good at the activity, you love doing it and you improve the condition of others. These activities are called the highest and best use of time. They build on your strengths, not on your weaknesses.

You can strategically maximize your highest and best use of time by continuously searching for ways to delegate, eliminate or outsource activities where you lack competence, don't feel passion or don't add value to others.

The 13 building blocks

You will need 13 building blocks to build your own incredible time machine. Each of these blocks will move you toward high performance by itself. Applied together, they have the power to make you unstoppable.

Clarity

Think of the incredible power of clarity. It triggers the subconscious part of your brain to become aware of people, ideas and circumstances to help you achieve your goals.

To get maximum clarity, for every meeting, project and action ask: what would success look like? Then describe and picture success as detailed as possible.

Project list

The subconscious part of your brain remembers every commitment you make with others and with yourself. However, this part of the brain has no sense of priority and time. For instance, every time you tell yourself you should wash the car, a part of your brain thinks you should be washing the car all the time. Your brain is a great goal-seeking machine and a brilliant planning machine. However, it is also a lousy secretary. That's why we need shopping lists.

A trick to make up for the brain's shortcomings in this area is to write down every single commitment with others and with yourself. This collection of commitments becomes your project list. Then, read through the list, making decisions on whether to eliminate or postpone each commitment. This exercise will then free your mind to focus on what it does best: goal seeking and planning.

Action list

Thinking is a high-energy activity. The brain, therefore, has a natural tendency to move quickly from a thinking hard state to a do-things-on-automatic-pilot state. To use your brain energy as efficiently as possible, it is best to batch your hard thinking.

Batching works as follows: think through your entire project list regularly, defining the smallest physical actions for each project. Then, write those actions on an action list and start executing them on autopilot. Once you have finished your action list, do this hard thinking exercise again. After a while you will begin to make enormous progress toward your goals.

Small steps

Once you have perfected your commitment list, you will notice that you are either attracted (buy a new car!) or repelled (clean the kitchen sink) by each project. The repulsive feelings are generated by the lizard part of the brain. This part associates change with uncertainty and risk and will do everything in its power to fight the change. The curious thing, however, is that the repulsive projects will often have the greatest positive impact on your life and your business.

To continue make progress on projects, here is a neat little trick. Imagine wild success for each project and define the smallest physical action you can take to make some progress. This exercise will lull your lizard brain to sleep (no risk in taking such a small step!) and all of a sudden you will start moving, even on the difficult projects.

Plan every day in advance

Planning your day in advance is one of the most powerful techniques to rapidly increase personal productivity. There are two reasons why this habit is effective to increase both your efficiency and your effectiveness. First, it forces you to step back each day and focus on activities that will help you most to make progress on your major goals.

Secondly, if you plan your next-day activities the evening before, the subconscious mind (the part of the brain that never sleeps) starts to work on these activities during the night. Often, you wake up with new and bright ideas to make the day really count.

Planning your day in advance is easy, as long as you commit to the following rules:

- Plan your next day the afternoon or evening before to max-

imize the idea-generation power of the subconscious mind.
- Plan on paper to increases the quality of the planning, checking off activities as you complete them. Each time you complete a task, you will experience a small endorphin rush. Endorphins are the natural wonder drugs of your brain, producing feelings of happiness and well-being.
- Avoid booking your calendar solid with wall-to-wall activities. Because surprises and emergencies occur daily, you want to build in some time to deal with unexpected events.

Pick three things and execute

When planning your day in advance, write down and resolve to complete three tasks, regardless of what the day throws at you. This habit alone will give you a sense of accomplishment at the end of each day and will motivate you to hold on to the habit of planning your day in advance.

Eat your frog

Embrace the habit of eating your frog first. This idea is that if you hypothetically start each day by eating a live frog, all tasks for the rest of the day will be a breeze.

Here is how to eat your frog:

- Start your working day making progress on your major goals, tackling the difficult, least attractive and often most important tasks first. If you have more than one frog, start with the ugliest one first. After you have eaten your ugly frog, the remainder of your activity list will look easy and will be much more fun to do.
- Do not stare at the frog; staring makes the frog grow bigger and uglier. Instead, move into action without much thought. After

completing the first five minutes of your most important task, you will have no problem continuing until you are finished.

if you hypothetically start each day by eating a live frog, all tasks for the rest of the day will be a breeze.

The two-minute rule

Your inbox is not your action list. In professional life, the ability to manage your inbox will usually give a huge boost to your productivity. Here's is a little trick: Apply the two-minute rule to all your incoming email; if you can do it within two minutes, do it now. Otherwise, schedule the action for a later time. Use an egg timer to ensure you stick to this rule. You will be surprised how many emails can suddenly be answered within two minutes.

Break Parkinson's Law

The most important rule for improving time use is to break Parkinson's Law. This law says that work expands so as to fill the time available for its completion. This law implies that you use the total scheduled amount of time to do a task. For instance, if you have scheduled a one-hour meeting, your team meets for one hour, regardless of whether you achieve the objectives of the meeting earlier than the allotted time.

However, breaking Parkinson's law will empower you to save significant amounts of time.

Here are two tips for breaking Parkinson's law:

- Schedule all your meetings in half of the usual time. You will notice that the meeting outcomes will be the same or even better. Nothing sharpens the mind more quickly than a pending deadline.
- The default position for planning a new meeting in Microsoft Outlook is one hour. Change the default, scheduling meetings to last only six minutes.

The deadline

The greatest invention of all time is the deadline. If deadlines didn't exist, no other invention would have ever taken place. The deadline imprints a sense of urgency in everything you do. It is the catalyst that translates potential into performance. Therefore, add a deadline to every project worth doing and move powerfully toward achieving your goals.

The zone

When you are interrupted from a task, research has shown it takes at least 10 minutes to refocus and continue.

Here are four practical ways of using this knowledge to your advantage to boost personal productivity:

- Single handle every task. Create the habit of sticking with a task until it is finished. There is a huge difference between 95 percent ready and 100 percent ready.

- Dedicate chunks of time in your calendar to work on your most important tasks and projects. Your brain has a certain time span after which it needs a short break to function optimally. This time span is called the zone. While the zone is different for each individual, it usually varies between 1 and 1.5 hours. Find your zone and create your chunks of time accordingly.

- Eliminate distractions while in the zone. Find a technique or tool such as headphones to help you block out external distractions. However, the greatest productivity killers are often internal distractions. To push away unrelated thoughts, have a pen and paper ready to write them down to review later.

- Switch off the email notification icon and commit to checking your email only twice a day at fixed times. There is a case study of a company that programmed its email server to deliver emails only twice a day at 10 a.m. and 4 p.m., achieving a company-wide productivity boost of at least 10 percent by doing so.

43 folders

What do you do with incoming "stuff" like minutes, notes, letters coupons and tickets? Usually it ends up in a pile of papers. Somehow you hope to remember what is in this pile when you need it in the future. Unfortunately, your brain isn't wired to remember things at the right place and at the right time. You need reminders, such as shopping lists for the supermarket.

However, there is a practical way to get away from building piles of stuff and have information in front of you at exactly the right moment. The solution is called a tickler system, or brain-forward system.

Here is how this system works:

Act!

- Take 43 file folders, labeling the first 31 with the numbers of the month, 1-31, and the remaining 12 with the name of each month, January through December.
- When you receive information that is relevant later in the month, store it in the appropriate file. For instance, if you receive the agenda of a meeting to be held on the 25th of that month, store the meeting agenda in the folder labeled 25.
- Every day, empty today's file folder into your inbox. For instance, if the month is October, empty the 6 folder on October 6th.
- When you receive information that is relevant later in the year, store it in the file of the month where you will need it. For instance, if you receive an invitation for a conference held in December, put the invitation into the file folder for December.
- On the first day of each month, open the file of this specific month and distribute the contents of this file in the daily file folders (numbered 1 to 31).

If you work with this system every day, you will create your own personal post office. Remember to work diligently on your post office, filing incoming stuff in the appropriate file folder and emptying the right folder into your inbox every day.

ABCDE method

The biggest waste of time isn't on doing things inefficiently, but spending time on things that shouldn't be done in the first place. Therefore, to maximize productivity, you must force yourself to prioritize. Prioritizing can be accomplished quickly using the ABCDE method.

First, before you start your day, divide your tasks into the following categories.

- A-tasks have significant consequences when not done (example: unhappy customers).
- B-tasks have only minor consequences when not done (example: upgrade your computer software).
- C-tasks have hardly any consequences when not done at all
  (example: socialize with your colleagues).
- D-tasks can be delegated to someone else (example: proofread
  a report).
- E-tasks should be eliminated anyway.

The next step is to prioritize all tasks inside the different categories (A-1, A-2, A-3, B-1, B-2, etc.). Then, work on each individual task in order, completing it before moving on to the next. This
forced priority system will help you make rapid progress on your
most important goals by working only on tasks that will produce
the highest return.

10

Why smart people do stupid things

Bernie Madoff pulled off one of the biggest Ponzi schemes in history. Using an elaborate system to pay off existing investors with money from new investors, he was able to run a facade of a successful investment firm for many years.

After its collapse, the most remarkable thing was not so much the Ponzi scheme itself, but the fact that his client list consisted of the elite of the elite in business. If it looks too good to be true, it probably is. Yet, Madoff attracted clients who were intelligent, successful and accomplished. So, how was it possible that so many smart people could be sucked into this obviously shady business?

This question is even more interesting, since the pattern of successful people en masse being fooled out of their money has been repeated many times throughout history. Recent examples are Enron and Worldcom. What is going on here?

One of the key principles of Peter Drucker, arguably the most influential business thinker of the twentieth century, is accurate thinking. Jack Welch, former GE CEO, famously took this observation to heart and adopted the habit of starting his meetings with one question: what is the reality?

Yet, in spite of best practices, many successful people often suffer from specific thinking biases. These biases pose huge risks for individuals, teams and companies and if not recognized and addressed, can ruin splendid reputations, shining careers and even well-regarded companies.

This chapter explores these anti-high-performance biases in more detail.

The Dunning-Kruger effect

The Dunning–Kruger effect is a phenomenon where people with little knowledge or skill think they know more or have more skill than they do. This means that people who are completely ignorant and unskilled in certain areas often overestimate how well they will perform in these areas. An example is playing golf. If you've never played golf, watching professional golf on television often invokes the reaction "how hard can it be?" Only when you hit your first round do you realize that playing golf requires a tremendous amount of skill. Everything is hard before it is easy, even for people who are already highly skilled in a particular area.

Needless to say, the Dunning-Kruger effect can wreak havoc on your best laid plans.

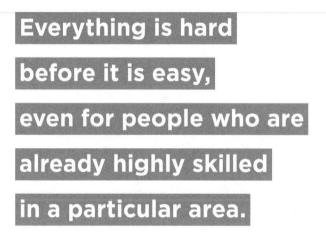

Everything is hard before it is easy, even for people who are already highly skilled in a particular area.

The God complex

A close cousin of the Dunning-Kruger effect is the God complex. If you are very good at one thing, you automatically think you are very good at many other things. This magnified image of self-worth explains why singers think they are good actors, actors think they are good politicians and politicians think they are good at everything.

Keep in mind that becoming skilled at something requires a lot of time. It also means you are lousy at everything else. Great talent invariably involves an enormous amount of weakness. This explains why accomplished athletes seldom win Noble prices and renowned captains of industry never become best-selling poetry authors.

The endowment effect

The human mind perceives the impact of losing something we already have to be greater than gaining something new. This so-called endowment effect means the impact of loss can be 10 times or more than the impact of gain. For instance, you would theoretically spend the same amount of energy to prevent a loss of $100 as you would spend to gain $1,000.

The endowment effect is especially prevalent when huge investments, such as in your finances or your reputation, have been made and additional investments are needed to move ahead. These investments are called sunk costs and pose a major obstacle to abandoning disastrous policies or projects. An example is Motorola's Iridium project from the late '90s, when ever-increasing investments in a hugely expensive satellite network were made to achieve global phone coverage, despite the rapid ascension of much cheaper cellular technology.

The Gell-Mann amnesia effect

The term Gell-Mann amnesia effect was first coined by the writer Michael Crichton. This effect works as follows. After opening a business magazine you stumble upon an article on some subject you know well, such as goal setting. After reading the article you conclude that the writer is clueless about the facts and issues. Then you turn the page to the next subject, and read as if the rest of the magazine were somehow more accurate about the other issues it covers.

The Gell-Mann amnesia effect is based on the idea that much of the information you absorb without question is inaccurate, compromised or even wrong. This knowledge puts a damper on your ability to innovate; much of what you know is simply not true, an awareness that leads to groupthink and confines your view of the world.

Thinking in reverse

When people, teams and organizations get stuck, they tend to either do more of the same things, or do less of the same things. This tendency is known as thinking in reverse. People prepare for the road ahead by looking in the rearview mirror. In many cases, this thinking bias is not helpful. To get results you never had before, you need to do things you have never done before. The best people, teams and organizations, therefore, force themselves to look for ways to do things differently.

It is dangerous to let past results influence future possibilities, especially in business. Remember Kodak? Nassim Taleb observed that a turkey is confident the butcher loves it for about a thousand days, since it is fed well and unmolested. Then Thanksgiving comes, and in the midst of a sense of great well-being, things change harshly. The past is not a very good predictor of the future, no matter how much data we have and how long we have it.

The dead horse fallacy

You never get the new results you want from the activities you like. (If this weren't the case, you would have gotten these results already.) People in business generally fall in love with approaches that have given them the best results in the past. However, since the world is constantly changing, what has gotten you here may no longer get you there. When faced with a new problem, your existing thinking patterns keep spewing out old solutions, before you realize they have become ineffective and obsolete. This thinking flaw is called the dead horse approach to solving problems.

When faced with a new problem, your existing thinking patterns keep spewing out old solutions, before you realize they have become ineffective and obsolete.

As an illustration of the dead horse fallacy, one day, a company catering to tourists, using horse and carriage for sightseeing, found that its only horse had died overnight. The management team convened and in a special meeting discussed what to do.

- The chief financial officer pointed out that a dead horse has a lower cost of ownership than a living horse. He therefore requested to use only dead horses from now on.

- The human resource director proposed a new bonus incentive program for the horse to increase its performance.
- The operations director ignored the dead horse, since dead was not listed as a viable entry for a horse in the SAP system.
- The patent attorney wondered whether the dead horse could be turned into a trademark.
- The legal officer argued the meaning of dead.
- The research director concluded more tests were required to determine if the horse was really dead.
- The communications officer considered the situation a great opportunity to launch a social media campaign to proudly highlight the merits of dead horses.
- In the end, after listening to these ideas, the CEO decided to form a committee to study the subject of dead horses.
- This story illustrates the folly of mindlessly sticking to old solutions and familiar approaches, when a new approach is called for.

The SETI fallacy

SETI stands for search for extraterrestrial intelligence. SETI is a program where scientists, using sophisticated equipment, look for evidence of intelligent life outside our planet. It has been going on for more than 50 years. So far, no luck.

If you ask the scientists involved in SETI if intelligent life outside our planet exists, they would invariably tell you that it does. Based on this viewpoint, you could easily conclude that science overwhelmingly concludes that humans are not alone in the universe. After all, you have been polling the most knowledgeable people on this subject, haven't you?

We'd still be wrong, because becoming an expert in any subject requires a passion for and belief in the subject. SETI scientists have become experts in extraterrestrial life, because they believe in it. Otherwise, they wouldn't spend their entire lives trying to prove something that doesn't exist. The same is true, for instance, for economists who believe in the predictive power of their economic models. They are all invested in the relevance of their calling.

This SETI thinking fallacy is dangerous for decision making in business. If you rely only on subject matter experts for predictive power, especially in a competitive subject field, you invariably rely on the true believers who have a passion for their subject. For instance, suppose while looking into opportunities to invest in energy, you turn to solar energy experts. No doubt these experts would make the business case for the great advantages of solar over any other energy source.

The way to overcome the SETI fallacy is to ask the following question to any subject expert: "what would need to happen for you to dismiss your recommendation?" Subject experts who can't answer this question suffer from groupthink. It has become a religion. If they can't answer this question, actively start looking for evidence elsewhere. Use experts outside your field to get it.

The pre-mortem

The thinking fallacies discussed so far are often the root of failure. Is there anything you can do to prevent these failures? While it's hard to recognize our own inaccurate thinking, we can easily spot this flaw in others. One of the most powerful ways to combat fatal thinking fallacies is therefore to invite the perspective from others by conducting a pre-mortem to determine causes of failure up front.

Failure often occurs because of what we think we know that simply isn't true. These flawed thoughts are known as assumptions, and they often cause great projects to crash and burn.

Conducting a pre-mortem on your project will help you avoid falling in this trap. A pre-mortem is the opposite of a project post-mortem. A post-mortem identifies mistakes after a project has failed. In a pre-mortem, however, you identify the major causes of project failure in a creative way before the start of a project by imagining the project has already failed. This exercise enables you to anticipate roadblocks beforehand and significantly increase the success rate of your endeavor.

Failure often occurs because of what we think we know that simply isn't true.

Here is how a pre-mortem team exercise works:
- Imagine five years in the future. Your project has failed so miserably that you you've been asked for an interview by the Harvard Business Review to talk about the reasons for your failure.
- The project team divides into small subgroups to discuss what would be said in this interview.
- All subgroups then report on their insights. The total feedback will give a clear picture of the main internal project

risks. Steps to mitigate these risks can then be incorporated into the project design from the start.

If you conduct a pre-mortem with a group of external subject experts, you will also quickly identify not only the main risks, but also the hidden opportunities. This knowledge will often be a great eye opener and will be invaluable to almost guarantee project success.

Sustainable high performance

There is a difference between self-confidence and arrogance. Self-confidence means you're convinced you can create value for others. Arrogance is the belief you have nothing more to learn.

All seven thinking biases, such as the Dunning-Kruger, Endowment effect and God complex, are rooted in arrogance and smugness. Fortunately, by applying the pre-mortem antidote outlined in this chapter regularly, you can take effective countermeasures to prevent falling into these thinking traps. It makes the difference between accidental and sustainable high performance.

If you encounter one of these biases in others though, keep in mind the words of Mark Twain: "Never argue with ignorant people. They will bring you down to their level and then beat you with experience."

11
Final
thoughts

There are two very important questions in life:
- What do you want?
- How do you get it?

This book is for people who know exactly what they want: to get to the top of their profession or industry. It provides dozens of ideas to do things differently, grow your business and get you there in the easiest, fastest and most elegant way possible.

I've found three main hurdles that hold people back from taking massive action on new ideas and, more specifically, on many of the ideas presented in this book:

- **Yes, but my business/profession/organization is different**. Keep in mind that businesses or professions share many more similarities than differences. The opportunity is to find these similarities and accommodate new ideas to see how they can work. For example, the velvet rope approach to marketing can be applied by local mom-and-pop stores, as well as by large global businesses. Visiting my local jewelry shop requires an appointment, after which you may or may not receive an invitation before you are even allowed to enter the store. Not much different from the American Express black card, which is by invitation only. Both businesses are successful, because they attract the best customers as a result.

- **I'm simply not attracted to this idea**. You'll never get the new results you want from your existing favorite behavior/approaches/ideas. Ideas you don't like are usually the ones that will help you most to take the next step in your career or business. Therefore, make sure to consider every idea, even the ones you don't like, and think critically about how you would apply the ideas.

- **I can't possibly do that, because I will receive push-back, criticism or even scorn from my industry or professional peers**. If you do what everyone else is doing, you're not distinguishing yourself and you're probably stuck. Your business or career is about your success, not about peer accolades. Therefore, if you start to receive pushback while implementing a new idea, it could very well be a sign that you are on the right track: World War II bomber pilots already knew that the heaviest flak occurred when flying on top of the target.

Data suggests that approximately 3 percent of people, teams and organizations are able to achieve extraordinary things and become Preeminent in their industries or professional fields. By applying the ideas from this book, you can become part of this 3 percent. The alternative, of course, is that you become part of the 97 percent who, in the end, work for this 3 percent. From now on, the choice is completely yours.

What are you waiting for?

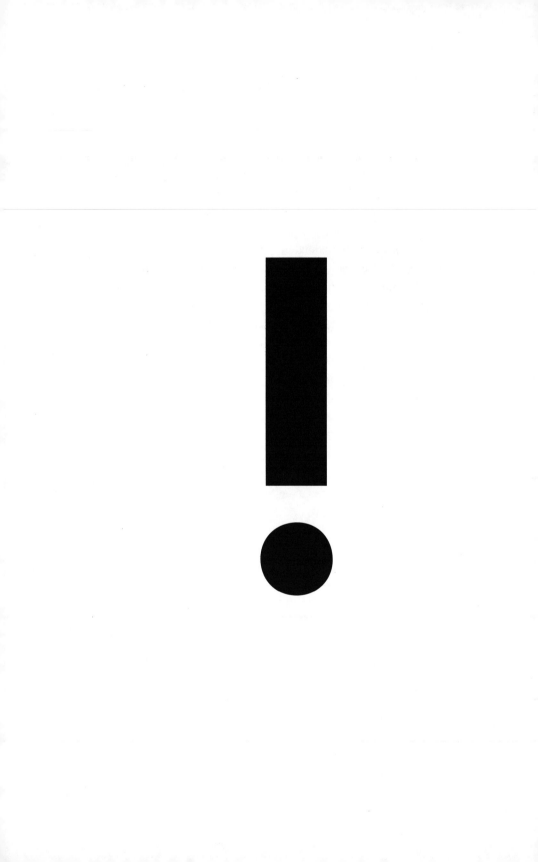

12

Getting started

Information is useless without taking action. Now is the time to get going: your achievements five years from now will be determined by the small and consistent actions you decide to take today.

Chapter 12

Enclosed are 30 ideas for small actions you can take immediately to move toward Preeminence. Pick the one you like most and get going. Motion beats meditation every time...

1 All change starts with a decision. Therefore, decide today to become Preeminent in your professional field. Define a small step to get there. Is it making a call, setting up a meeting or buying a book? Then take action immediately.

2 Imagine wild success! Create a vision board of what your business or career will look like five years from now.

3 Buy a notebook, a great pen and start to do the 10-goal exercise twice a day. This small investment of 10 minutes a day will have a massive impact on the speed in which you achieve your goals.

4 Change your reading habits. From now on, pick up magazines and books read by presidents, CEOs and other business leaders. A list of 50 great books can be found at the end of this book.

5 Set an ambitious professional goal to achieve this year. Then determine the three most important smart marketing, innovation and strategy approaches to get there in the fastest way possible.

6 Determine the key skill that is holding you back from becoming Preeminent. Then make a plan to acquire this skill in the fastest way possible.

7 Identify the leadership behavior that will have the greatest positive impact on achieving your goals. Is it connecting your vision to others, fostering collaboration or maybe setting a new professional standard? Once identified, decide to work on this behavior to become better every single day.

8 Determine the usual risk reversal strategy in your business and decide what you can do to massively improve on this strategy to delight existing clients and attract new clients.

9 Name the 5 push backs you hear most often when offering your product or your service. Then think of 10 comebacks you can use for each pushback.

10 Design a systematic process to get referrals from every client you do business with.

11 Make a list of everyone who has used your product or service in the past three years. Then reach out to these people, asking if you can be of service and if they know anyone else who might need your service or product.

12 Ask your best customers what they specifically like about you, your service or your product. Then emphasize this feedback in everything you do.

13 Set aside at least 20 percent of your time to engage in marketing activities. Try to increase this number gradually to 50 percent.

14 Ask yourself what nuisance is reluctantly being tolerated by clients in your industry. For example, waiting lines in a bank, or being herded like cattle in an airplane. Then think of ways to do things differently and delight your clients.

15 Rally a group of 5 to 8 people and conduct a workshop called "How to Destroy Your Business." Look for the most creative ways to run your existing business into the ground. Then take the most promising ideas and see what happens if you do exactly the opposite. This exercise might give rise to new and vastly innovative ideas.

16 When you accept a new project, quit at least two other projects to free up energy to get started with this new initiative.

17 Ask for the job or activities that you love to do. Often, others simply are not aware of your true passions at work.

18 Every year fire the bottom 20 percent of your customers. Give them to your competitors and use the newly released energy to replace these with new and better customers.

19 Open your next meeting with power: Attention, Information, Expectations, Engagement, Involvement.

20 Explain to your team how you would like to receive communication: for instance with the CLEAR model, or with know-feel-do (both techniques described in detail in this book).

21 More than 90 percent of your decisions are not important. Focus your time and energy on the 10 percent of decisions that truly matter. Spend minimal mental energy on the other 90 percent.

22 Decide to build a high-performance habit today. Define the desired behavior, then put five paperclips in your left pocket. Every time you show the desired behavior, move a paperclip from your left to your right pocket. At the end of the day, all five paperclips should be in your right pocket. Repeat for 21 days, and you have built the foundations of a new habit.

23 Which of the incredible time machine habits will have the biggest immediate impact on your performance? Set a goal to improve in the next 21 days on this item. Then move to the next goal.

Apply the concept of your Golden Hour (which is the time of the day that you are most productive) to work solely on your marketing and innovation activities during this time.

 Install a Board of Advisors for yourself or your company to ensure you bring in different perspectives. Buy them dinner every few months and listen carefully to what they have to say.

 Watch out for consensus. It usually means that the group has not given the issue enough thought. Reconvene at a later time to address the issue again.

Give this book as a present to someone else. Then discuss the most interesting content together and decide how you will help each other implement some of the ideas.

Identify the one idea from this book you dislike most. Then think about how you can modify this idea to make it actionable for you.

Make a conscious decision whether to raise your prices at least two times a year. When in doubt, raise your prices.

Listen to educational audiobooks while traveling. This is one of the fastest way to receive condensed wisdom in a very short time and become an expert in a subject as fast as possible.

50 books
to achieve
Preeminence

Chapter 1

Blink, Malcolm Gladwell (Back Bay Books 2007)

Brain Boosters, Win Wenger (Nightingale Conant, 2003)

Brain Rules, John Medina (Pear Press, 2009)

Brainsteering, Kevin P. Coyne (HarperBusiness, 2011)

The 7 Habits of Highly Effective People, Stephen R. Covey (Free Press, 1990)

The Goal Achiever, Bob Proctor (Life Success Productions, 2001)

The Magic of Thinking Big, David J. Schwartz (Fireside, 1987)

Think and Grow Rich, Napoleon Hill (TarcherPerigee, 2005)

Unlimited Power, Anthony Robbins (Free Press, 2008)

Your Brain at Work, David Rock (HarperCollins, 2009)

Chapter 2

Built to Last, Jim Collins (HarperBusiness, 2004)

Strategic Acceleration, Tony Jeary (Vanguard Press, 2010)

The Effective Executive, Peter F. Drucker (HarperBusiness, 2006)

The E-myth Revisited, Michael E. Gerber (HarperCollins, 1995)

The Sticking Point Solution, Jay Abraham (Perseus Books Group, 2009)

What the CEO Wants You to Know, Ram Charan (Random House Inc, 2001)

Chapter 3

Influence, Robert Cialdini (Harper Business, 2006)

No B.S. Business Success, Dan Kennedy (Entrepreneur Press, 2004)

The 80/20 Principle, Richard Koch (Nicholas Brealey Publishing, 2011)

Chapter 4

Book Yourself Solid, Michael Port (Wiley, 2010)

Duct Tape Marketing, John Jantsch (Thomas Nelson, 2008)

Rain Making, Ford Harding (Adams Media, 2008)

The Ultimate Sales Machine, Chet Holmes (Portfolio, 2007)

Chapter 5

Goals!, Brian Tracy (Berrett-Koehler Publishers, 2010)

Hard Goals, Mark Murphy (McGraw-Hill Education, 2010)

Omdenken, the Dutch art of flip-thinking, Berthold Gunster (Lev., 2016)

Simplicity, Edward de Bono (Penguin UK, 2010)

The Genius Code, Paul Scheele and Win Wenger (Learning Strategies Corporation, 2002)

Chapter 6

Do the Work, Steven Pressfield (The Domino Project/Black Irish Entertainment, 2014)

The Dip, Seth Godin (Piatkus, 2011)

The Little Big Things, Tom Peters (HarperStudio, 2010)

The Power of Full Engagement, Jim Loehr and Tony Schwartz (Free Press, 2003)

Chapter 7

Accelerated Learning Techniques, Colin Rose and Brian Tracy (Nightingale Conant, 2005)

Million Dollar Consulting, Alan Weiss (McGraw-Hill Education, 2009)

Talent is Overrated, Geoff Colvin (Nicholas Brealey Publishing, 2011)

The New Rational Manager, Charles H. Kepner (Princeton Research Press, December 1997)

Chapter 8

Enchantment, Guy Kawasaki (Portfolio Penguin, 2011)

How to Win Every Argument, Madsen Pirie (Continuum, 2007)

Iconoclast, Gregory Berns Ph.D. (Harvard Business Review Press, 2010)

Made to Stick, Chip Heath and Dan Heath (Cornerstone Digital, 2008)

The Debater's Guide, Jon Ericson (Southern Illinois University Press, 1987)

The Simplicity Survival Handbook, Bill Jensen (Basic Books, 2007)

The Ultimate Book of Mind Maps, Tony Buzan (Thorsons Publishers, 2006)

What Got You Here Won't Get You There, Marshall Goldsmith (Profile Books, 2010)

Chapter 9

Execution, Larry Bossidy (Crown Pub, 2009)

Getting Things Done, David Allen (Penguin, 2001)

The 4-Hour Workweek, Timothy Ferriss (Crown Publishers, Inc., 2007)

The Success Principles™, Jack Canfield (William Morrow Paperbacks, 2015)

Chapter 10

Black Swan, Nassim Taleb (Random House Trade Paperbacks, 2010)

Thinking, Fast and Slow, Daniel Kahneman (Farrar, Straus and Giroux, 2011)

Acknowledgments

My gratitude to Josefine van Zanten, Thierry Muller and Vineeta Yadav, professionals extraordinaire. We have shown that a single pebble thrown in the ocean can change the shore line.

Thank you Richard Habets, Jan Scheele and Jan-Willem Sanders, for inspiring me to always think big.

My thanks to Dorseda de Block, who, as the editor of the original English version, used her profound language skills to make an invaluable contribution to this book.

Freek Talsma and Douwe van Randen from Vakmedianet: it has been a great experience working with all of you.

Thank you Douwe Hoendervanger for the outstanding book design.

And mostly for my wife Francesca, and Matteo and Elisabetta, my children. You constantly remind me that life is about family and bringing value to others. All else is just commentary.

About the author

How do the best get better? Paul Rulkens knows that 'doing more' is no longer the default answer to 'too much to do.' He is an expert in high performance: the art and science of accelerating bold executive outcomes with the least amount of effort. He is an award-winning professional speaker, author and a trusted boardroom advisor who has helped thousands of business owners, professionals and executives get everything they can out of everything they have. His ideas to improve results and accelerate careers are often described as thought-provoking and counter-intuitive, yet highly effective.

You do not have to be sick in order to get better. As an international keynote speaker, Paul annually addresses dozens of successful international audiences about essential mindsets and proven strategies to reap exponential improvements. His most popular topics cover the secrets of consistent execution, easy innovation, powerful leadership, growth focus and seamless teamwork.

Originally trained as a chemical engineer, Paul's work is based on deep knowledge and extensive experience in the practical business applications of behavioral psychology, neuroscience and, especially, common sense. His popular TED talks are used frequently in professional training sessions all over the world.

About the author

His clients call his keynotes both substantive and hilarious. The reason may be that Paul once was trained as a standup comedian, receiving critical acclaim for his Arnold Schwarzenegger impersonation. However, the miserable failure of his ensuing 'pumping iron' muscle development project prevented him from pursuing his true calling in life: a career as a credible Arnold Schwarzenegger body double ...

Contact:
Paul Rulkens, Agrippa Consulting International
(Maastricht, The Netherlands)
paul@agrippaci.com
+31 6 37604168
www.agrippaci.com

Index

Index

Index

Y

Z